the
101
BEST FREELANCE CAREERS

the
101
BEST FREELANCE CAREERS

Kelly Reno

Berkley Books, New York

Kind permission was granted by Harry Frisch for material excerpted from his book *How to Be a Supersalesman . . . and Still Respect Yourself in the Morning* appearing in Chapter Four.

This book is an original publication of The Berkley Publishing Group.

THE 101 BEST FREELANCE CAREERS

A Berkley Book / published by arrangement with
the author

PRINTING HISTORY
Berkley trade paperback edition / June 1999

The Penguin Putnam Inc. World Wide Web site address is http://www.penguinputnam.com

ISBN: 0-425-16865-4

BERKLEY®
Berkley Books are published by The Berkley Publishing Group, a division of Penguin Putnam Inc., 375 Hudson Street, New York, New York 10014.
BERKLEY and the "B" design are trademarks belonging to Penguin Putnam Inc.

PRINTED IN THE UNITED STATES OF AMERICA

10 9 8 7 6 5 4 3 2 1

This book is dedicated to my grandmother, Betty Hart-O'Rourke, for her encouragement, love and belief in me. Thank you for passing along the "O'Rourke Family Writing Gene."

Contents

introduction

freelance \\'frē-lan(t)s\\ · working by the hour, day or job, selling services or work independently to clients rather than working as a salaried employee.

career \\kə-'rir\\ · an occupation or profession that is how one earns a living or one's life work. The word "career" is derived from the Old French word *carrière*, which means "road." A career is thus a road that one takes on one's travels through life.

Welcome to the era of the self-employed. We live in uncertain times and are no longer able to depend upon our employers for job security as our parents and grandparents did.

Corporations and businesses of all sizes, attempting to reduce expenses and overhead, are constantly "downsizing" their in-house employees and trimming personnel departments, from the most junior secretary to top executives. The good news is that many of these corporations and businesses are now hiring freelance professionals to handle projects and workloads outside of the office.

No jobs are secure except those of the self-employed.

If you're working, ask yourself these questions:

· How stable is your job?

- Will your job even exist in ten years, and if so, will you be making the kind of money you need and want there?
- Do you ever wish that you could be your own boss and be in complete control of your financial destiny?

Self-employed people make up a small percentage of our workforce, but the numbers continue to rise every year. Self-employed people may not have careers that keep them surefire safe from the unemployment lines, but these people are tough and able to accept and roll with our changing times. Self-employed people can see opportunity and are able to jump on the bandwagon, sometimes changing careers every few years to pursue more lucrative professions as the times allow. Freelancers are thinkers and don't let little things like depressed economies and lack of newspaper want ads stop them. They *create* their own jobs, security and future. Freelancers make the decisions and operate as their own bosses. Freelancers have freedom and independence from employers, and the opportunity to enjoy work that is personally satisfying. Freelancing can be done on a part-time or full-time basis depending upon how much time you have available or are willing to dedicate to your career. This new breed of workers is taking America by storm.

Freelance professionals must treat their careers as businesses. Anyone looking to become a freelancer to live the easy life has got the wrong idea. Freelancing takes discipline, hard work and more hard work to get your business off the ground. Sure, you may be able to make a great living, maybe even become very wealthy, but you will only get from your career what you are willing to give to it.

The purpose of this book is to introduce you to the wide-open world of opportunity available for freelance professionals. I hope to enlighten you about new ways to make a living and how to be your own boss on your own terms.

INTRODUCTION

In this book, you will find 101 of the best careers for freelance professionals. Some of the careers are unusual, even unheard of, but never the less, they are all some of the best ways I've found to make money. I hope to reveal new possibilities to you and have tried to list something for virtually everyone. I hope that you find your perfect career within these pages or that this book will lead you to find your own dream career. The careers listed in this book are *real* professions that *real* people are making a living with.

Read this book to find out

- What the hottest careers are
- What kind of work is involved with each career
- What skills, knowledge and training you need for each career
- What organizations, schools, suppliers and publications can help to get you started

This information and much, much more is revealed in the pages to follow. I wish you many successes with your new freelance career!

Do You Have What It Takes to Be a Freelance Professional?

Today's changing workplace is an unstable place to be. If you're one of the ones fortunate enough to be holding a job, ask yourself these questions:

· Are you truly happy and satisfied with your work?
· Are you earning the salary you deserve?
· Will your job exist in five years?

If you answered no to or were uncertain about any of the questions, you should definitely consider joining the millions of self-employed Americans who are working for themselves as freelance professionals.

Most freelance professionals work from home and have flexible schedules. Freelance professionals also have the opportunity to make as much money as they want and only have to look to themselves for raises and promotions.

Inside the pages of this book, you will discover the hidden job market. The freelance careers listed in this book are jobs that are always available, because you *create* them. You can begin preparing for a new career today and forget about working for someone else.

ARE YOU READY TO BE A FREELANCE PROFESSIONAL?

Freelance professionals are one of the fastest growing groups in the American workforce. This test was specially designed to help you discover if you're ready to start a freelance career.

THE FREELANCE TEST

TRUE OR FALSE

Read these statements and answer each with an honest true, false or undecided.

1. I can plan out and complete projects when I want to.
2. I'd prefer that someone else make decisions for me.
3. I'm a good listener.
4. The thought of change upsets me.
5. My time is valuable.
6. My viewpoint is very important.
7. I'm usually nice and courteous to other people.
8. Without a formal education, you can't make a lot of money.
9. I consider myself to be a creative person.
10. Others often ask me for advice.
11. I usually keep my promises.
12. I'm a fast learner.
13. I'm usually on time for appointments.
14. I don't work well on deadlines.
15. Taking risks scares me.
16. I have confidence in myself.
17. No one understands me.
18. I can usually communicate ideas clearly to others.
19. I usually know what I'm talking about.
20. I am able to keep myself on a strict schedule.

MULTIPLE CHOICE

Read each question and answer by circling a, b, c, d or e.

1. I take a freelance job for a high-paying client and discover in the middle of the job that the client is doing something unethical. I would

   a. Ignore it and finish the job as fast as possible
   b. Call the law authorities immediately
   c. Pretend I didn't see anything and continue taking other freelance assignments from the client (After all, the pay is really good.)
   d. Confront the client and let him know that I will not tolerate unethical activity, and leave if it continues
   e. I don't know

2. On my first job, I run into technical problems and am having difficulties completing the work. I would

   a. Quickly get the technical know-how (if possible) and complete the job satisfactorily
   b. Fake my way through and hope that the client didn't notice
   c. Call in an expert in the field in which I was having problems and "eat it" profitwise
   d. Tell the client that I couldn't complete the work and leave
   e. I don't know

3. An important client wants a second bid for a job and calls me. The bid she has is obviously underpriced. I would

   a. Offer the client an even lower price even though I'll barely make a profit
   b. Explain to the client why my price would be higher and let her know that I'll do a better job

   c. Laugh at the first bid and tell the client that the guy who quoted her that price was an idiot

   d. Tell the client that I'll match the price of the original bid and get her agreement to use me for future jobs if she's satisfied with my work

   e. I don't know

4. I've just completed a job for a client and he says he doesn't have the money to pay me even though the work was done satisfactorily. I would

   a. Threaten him with legal collection actions

   b. Meet with him and discuss how we might work out a payment plan

   c. Forget about it and move on to the next job

   d. Decide that from here on out I will get clients to pay me in advance

   e. I don't know

5. I've been studying information to start my new career and it is causing me a considerable amount of difficulty timewise. I would

   a. Continue studying anyway; I really want to change my life

   b. Drop my studies until life allows me the time to continue

   c. Choose another career that I can start immediately without the hassle

   d. Study when I have the time even though it might take a little longer

   e. I don't know

6. I've been operating as a freelance professional on a part-time basis while holding a full-time job as a secretary. I get a call from a major client who wants to hire me to do a really big

job that pays very well, but would require me to work full-time. I would

a. Quit my secretary job and go for it! (This is the break I've been waiting for.)
b. Decline the job offer (My secretary paycheck is small, but I'm afraid to quit and lose the security.)
c. Take a leave of absence from my secretary job and accept the freelance job
d. Decline the offer, but continue to work on a part-time basis as a freelance professional for other clients as my schedule allows
e. I don't know

7. I make an agreement with a client to do a job for a set price and discover halfway through the job that I have had under-bid it. I would

a. Complete the job satisfactorily anyway and learn from the experience
b. Tell the client that I would have to charge more than we originally agreed on and try to talk her into paying me more for my extra time
c. Overcharge another client to make up for my losses on this job
d. Rush to get the job done and give the client a so-so result or product that he won't necessarily notice
e. I don't know

8. I've been doing freelance work for a client who pays me fairly and offers me work on a regular basis. Suddenly, I get an offer to work from a big client who offers me triple my regular salary on a project. If I take the new job, I'll have to set back my regular client's current job. I would

a. Take the new job and make up an excuse to tell the regular client about why I need more time to finish his job
b. Accept the new job and make sure I get both jobs done, although it won't be easy to make enough time for both
c. Quit working for the regular client and start on the new job (The pay is so much better.)
d. Decline the new offer and remain loyal to my regular client
e. I don't know

9. If I'm going to make money as a freelance professional, I'll have to

a. Charge clients a lot of money for my services
b. Be lucky and hope that things go well
c. Work hard and charge fair prices
d. Spend at least five years getting trained in my profession
e. I don't know

10. If I overslept one morning and was going to be late for an appointment with a client, I would

a. Call the client, apologize for the inconvenience and get there as soon as possible
b. Throw my alarm clock at the wall
c. Make up a story about getting stuck in traffic
d. Offer the client a small discount to make up for the inconvenience
e. I don't know

TEST SCORING

Each answer on the test has a number value. After answering the questions, add up your total number of points to get your score.

True or False

1. T-1, F-0
2. T-0, F-1
3. T-1, F-0
4. T-0, F-1
5. T-1, F-0
6. T-1, F-0
7. T-1, F-O
8. T-0, F-1
9. T-1, F-0
10. T-1, F-0
11. T-1, F-0
12. T-1, F-0
13. T-1, F-0
14. T-0, F-1
15. T-0, F-1
16. T-1, F-0
17. T-0, F-1
18. T-1, F-0
19. T-1, F-0
20. T-1, F-0

Multiple Choice

1. A-3, B-1, C-2, D-4, E-0
2. A-4, B-1, C-3, D-2, E-0
3. A-2, B-4, C-1, D-3, E-0
4. A-2, B-4, C-1, D-3, E-0
5. A-4, B-1, C-2, D-3, E-0
6. A-4, B-1, C-3, D-2, E-0
7. A-3, B-4, C-1, D-2, E-0
8. A-2, B-4, C-1, D-3, E-0
9. A-3, B-4, C-1, D-2, E-0
10. A-4, B-1, C-2, D-3, E-0

TEST EVALUATION

46 POINTS AND UP

Congratulations! You are a natural freelance professional. You possess a good understanding of responsibility, leadership and integrity. You have an optimistic outlook in life and will have many successes. You are ready to make a new start.

30–45 POINTS

You are on the right track and have a pretty good sense of ethics and responsibility, but could use some good advice to perfect what you already know. You strive to be successful, but find yourself getting into trouble from time to time in life. Read the sections of this book about working for yourself and on integrity and take the test again.

25 POINTS OR BELOW

Don't worry that you scored in the lower point range of the test. You are already ahead of most people because you have made efforts to better your life by looking into starting a new career. Being responsible and using common sense to make decisions play key roles in determining your failures or successes. Hard work, integrity and being willing to learn are three important things that you need to remember and apply to turn things around.

HOW TO GET WHAT YOU WANT

This special section was designed to help you discover exactly what your goals are, how to attain them, and to help you isolate problems and develop solutions.

SECTION ONE

Answer the following questions with descriptive words.

1. Describe the kind of person you'd like to be.

_____

_____

_____

_____

_____

_____

2. Describe the kind of life you'd like to live.

_____

_____

_____

_____

_____

3. What do you want from a career?

_____

_____

_____

_____

_____

4. What admirable qualities do your mentors possess?

_____

_____

_____

_____

_____

_____

5. Describe your ideal life.

_____

_____

_____

_____

_____

_____

SECTION TWO

What changes do you need to make to get your life from here (present time) to your ideal life? Fill in the blanks relating to your

Career

_____

_____

_____

Family

_____

_____

_____

Financial Situation

_____

_____

_____

Personality

_____

_____

_____

Problems

_____

_____

_____

Bad Situations

_____

_____

_____

Health

_____

_____

_____

Other

_____

_____

_____

SECTION THREE

Answer these questions about yourself by filling in the blanks. Your answers will serve as available resources for solving problems and obtaining your goals in life.

1. My positive personality traits are

_____

_____

_____

2. I'm good at

_____

_____

_____

3. I like

_____

_____

_____

4. I'm interested in

_____

_____

_____

5. People who like and/or love me are (list names)

_____

_____

_____

6. I find happiness in

_____

_____

_____

7. My skills are

_____

_____

_____

8. I am knowledgeable about

_____

_____

_____

Now that you've filled out the answer sections, take a look at section one. This is your ideal life, what you dream of having, becoming and being. In order to possess the traits in section one and to work toward having your ideal life, you need to use what attributes and resources you have available. These attributes and resources are the things you've listed in section three. Take what you've got (from section three) and use it to make the necessary changes in section two. This is a standard formula you can use when making a plan to obtain goals.

TRY ON A CAREER

When we buy clothing, we usually try on different sizes, styles and colors before we buy. Does the garment fit right? Is it comfortable? Is it made to last or is it just a fad? A new career can be compared to an important garment such as a wedding dress. You've got to try it on and make sure it's perfect in every way before you make that big, important purchase.

The following test will serve as your dressing room for new career ideas. Filling in the blanks will act as your dressing-room mirror.

*This section can be photocopied as many times as you like. Try on as many careers as you want, as you would try on many outfits!

Career title

_____

_____

_____

What are the duties of this career?

_____

_____

_____

What would I like about this career?

_____

_____

_____

What might I dislike about this career?

_____

_____

_____

Would this career allow me to make the kind of money I need
and want?

_____

_____

_____

Would I still enjoy this career in five years?

_____

_____

_____

Why am I attracted to this career?

_____

_____

_____

Why would I be good at this career?

_____

_____

_____

Am I physically able to do this type of work?

_____

_____

_____

What skills or knowledge do I already have that are related to this career?

_____

_____

_____

Would I need training for this career?

_____

_____

_____

If yes, what formal training (school) would I need, or can I apprentice?

_____

_____

_____

Who or what organizations do I need to contact for more data and/or training?

_____

_____

_____

How long until I can start this new career?

_____

_____

_____

Would I choose to start this career full-time or part-time?

_____

_____

_____

Now that you've filled out this section for careers that you are interested in, look over your answers. Do the plus points outweigh the negative points? Do the above exercise with several careers, until you find your perfect career match.

The 101 Best Freelance Careers

In this chapter, 101 of today's hottest freelance careers have been highlighted and discussed, with valuable information given about how to get started in each.

*The amount of money a freelance professional can make and success with each career depends upon the individual.

· ACUPRESSURIST ·

Career Description

Acupressure is a natural, healing therapy that helps the body release tension. Acupressure was developed in China thousands of years ago when it was discovered that applying pressure to certain points of the body provided relief from injuries and illness. These discoveries were perfected over the years into modern acupressure. An acupressurist is an individual who practices acupressure techniques.

Career Opportunities

Most acupressurists have their own private practices and some work for natural healing centers. Acupressure is often used in addition to other healing therapies such as massage, midwifery, chiropractic, naturopathy and even acupuncture.

Training

Acupressurists must complete a training program. Some states require that acupressurists carry a touch therapist license, but others require no licensing. See the Massage Therapist entry for more information.

For more information contact

The American Oriental Bodywork Therapy Association
Laurel Oak Corporate Center, Suite 408
1010 Haddonfield Berlin Road
Vorhees, NJ 08043
(609) 782-1616
List of approved acupressure training programs

Emperor's College of Traditional Oriental Medicine
1807-B Wilshire Blvd.
Santa Monica, CA 90403
(310) 453-8300
Acupressure training programs and extension courses

Mueller College of Holistic Studies
4607 Park Blvd.
San Diego, CA 92116-2630
1-800-245-1976, (619) 291-9811
Acupressure training program

Recommended Reading

Acupressure: A Practical Introduction to the Benefits of This Therapy, Carola Beresford-Cooke, Macmillan, 1996

Acupressure for Everybody, Cathryn Bauer, Henry Holt and Company, 1991

· ANTIQUES APPRAISER ·

Career Description

An antiques appraiser is a person who can determine the correct value of antiques. Appraisers know the current market prices and keep up with collecting trends. A good appraiser is able to tell the difference between a replica and the real thing and can determine in what period or year a piece was made based on its style and markings.

Career Opportunities

Many people collect antiques for their beauty, rarity and sentimental value. An antique is an item that is over one hundred years old, but many items are called antiques or collectibles even through they are not quite that old. Every year, the value of an antique can go up, due to age and collecting trends. It can be a difficult task to determine the approximate value of an item to the average person, and appraisers are often hired to do the job.

Most antiques appraisers specialize in only a few areas, such as jewelry, china, dolls, furniture or particular types of collectible memorabilia, such as The Beatles or Coca-Cola. Since there are so many types of antiques and collectibles, appraisers tend to stick to the items they know best. It is easier to become an expert in a few chosen areas, rather than trying to know everything about everything. Yearly antiques price guides are released on almost every type of antique. Appraisers use these guides and also visit antiques shows and shops to get an all-around feel for the correct price of an item.

Some appraisers work in antiques shops, while others do house calls. This career can be done on a part-time basis and offers a good opportunity to get into the business of dealing antiques.

Expert appraisers know a good deal when they find one and can make some extra money by locating and selling items to their collecting clients. Your potential clients will include private individuals and collectors, antiques dealers and auction houses. If you are asked to appraise an antique that you are not familiar with, you may contact antiques shops and dealers to find out what they think it's worth, and you should look up the item in a price guide as well, to come up with an approximate value.

Training

There is no training required to become an antiques appraiser. To get started, pick two or three categories of antiques that you would like to specialize in, such as silver and dolls or coins and furniture. Buy the price guides for those categories and study them. Go out to antiques shops and locate some items and see if they are selling below or above the market value. Contact collector's clubs and subscribe to their newsletters and leave your business cards at antiques shops and with people at antiques shows.

When asking antiques dealers what they think an item is worth, be aware that they may give you a lower quote than it's actual value in hopes that they can acquire it at a low price.

Recommended Reading

Antiques & Auction News, Route 230 West, P.O. Box 500, Mount Joy, PA 17552, (717) 653-1833—Weekly tabloid for antiques dealers

Collectors News & The Antique Reporter, P.O. Box 156, Grundy Center, IA 50638-0156, (319) 824-6981—Monthly tabloid covering antiques, collectibles and nostalgic memorabilia

Treasure Chest, The Information Source & Marketplace for Collectors and Dealers of Antiques, Venture Publishing Company, Richmond Square, Suite 215E, Providence, RI 02906, (800) 557-9662—Monthly newspaper on antiques and collectibles

· AROMATHERAPIST ·

Career Description

Aromatherapy is the practice of using richly aromatic essential oils extracted from plants, herbs and flowers to relieve mental and physical ailments. The term "aromatherapy" was coined in the 1920s, but the practice dates as far back as 4500 B.C. and was used by the ancient Greeks, Romans and Egyptians. This natural healing art uses oils extracted from plants to regulate the body and ease the mind.

Career Opportunities

Modern-day aromatherapists use essential oils for many purposes, such as stress relief, calming, weight loss, and energizing. The therapeutic effect of these oils is achieved by absorption through the skin or inhalation. Oils can be combined with lotions, bath oils or even added to the water in vaporizers.

Only pure essential oils should be used when practicing aromatherapy. Synthetic fragrances may smell nice, but have no beneficial value to the human body. Essential oils can be purchased from health food stores and there are many books on the practice and uses of the oils.

Aromatherapists are familiar with the benefits and proper usage of essential oils and recommend the use of the appropriate oils to their clients. For example, a whiff of essential orange oil can help to cheer someone up and a few drops of lavender essential oil added to the bath can help to calm and relax. There are many essential oils that are used alone or in combination to help clients with various problems. The practice of aromatherapy is often incorporated with massage by adding beneficial oils to the massage oil. See the Massage Therapist entry for more information.

Aromatherapy is a relatively new practice in the United States, which leaves plenty of room for new aromatherapists. Some aromatherapists work in salons, while others operate their own private practices.

Training

Aromatherapists are not required to have a license. Training is available and there are many books available on the subject of essential oils and their uses.

For more information contact

Aroma Vera
5901 Rodeo Road
Los Angeles, CA 90016-4312
1-800-669-9514
Aromatherapy home study course, supplies, books

The Clayton School of Natural Healing
2140 11th Avenue South, #305
Birmingham, AL 35205
1-800-995-4590
Natural healing correspondence courses

Recommended Reading

The Illustrated Encyclopedia of Essential Oils: The Complete Guide to the Use of Oils in Aromatherapy and Herbalism, Julia Lawless, Element Books, 1995

Practical Art of Aromatherapy, Deborah Nixon, Crescent Books, 1995

Rodale's Illustrated Encyclopedia of Herbs, Rodale Press, Inc., 1987

· BODYGUARD ·

Career Description

A bodyguard is a person hired to physically protect another, usually a celebrity or high official, from bodily harm.

Career Opportunities

There are two types of bodyguards employed today. The first is the high-profile type we usually think of when we hear the term "bodyguard." A high-profile bodyguard is a person in excellent physical condition who escorts his or her employer in plain sight to intimidate and discourage physical attacks. A good example of this type of guard is the large bodybuilder often seen within close range of a celebrity. High profiles must know defense tactics and must be able to think fast to avoid harm to their employers. Some bodyguards are permitted to carry weapons. This is a good career for a fitness buff who enjoys exciting and challenging work.

The second type of bodyguard is the low-profile type. The low profiles usually look and dress like ordinary people and go about their business unnoticed. Low profiles may evaluate situations for security dangers and blend into the background, but always have their employers in mind. An example of a low profile's work would be checking out a hotel for possible security risks before an employer checks in. Some of these duties could be planning alternate entrance and exit routes from the building, checking for hidden microphones or cameras and ensuring privacy from fans or unwanted members of the press. A low-profile bodyguard must be an expert in security measures and may be permitted to carry a weapon.

Training

A military, police or security background is a plus in this career, but not mandatory. If you want to become a high-profile bodyguard, you should be in excellent physical condition and have training in martial arts or other defensive training. To be a low-profile bodyguard, you need to learn about undercover work, security countermeasures, surveillance and shadowing.

For more information contact

> The Nick Harris Detective Academy
> 16917 Enadia Way
> Van Nuys, CA 91406
> 1-800-642-5427
> Private investigator training

> West Coast Detective Academy
> 5113 Lankershim Blvd.
> North Hollywood, CA 91601
> 1-800-752-5555
> Security and undercover training

· BOOKKEEPER ·

Career Description

A bookkeeper is a person who keeps accounting records of money for businesses or private individuals.

Career Opportunities

Every business must keep financial records, from the smallest store to the largest corporation. Many freelance bookkeepers work for small- to medium-sized businesses who don't require full-time help. The bookkeeper comes in once a week or twice a month to organize and update the accounting records.

Bookkeepers usually have several clients at any given time, which keeps them working on a full-time basis. Every city has many small businesses, which leaves no shortage of work for professional bookkeepers. Your clients may be doctors, dentists, retail stores, restaurants, service companies, churches, private schools, law firms, real estate agencies, hotels and a wide variety of other businesses. Bookkeepers also work for individuals, organizing their personal financial records.

Some of the services bookkeepers may provide for their clients are totaling assets and liabilities, revenues and expenses, and debits and credits; balancing books; collecting accounts receivable; financial reporting; budgeting; petty cash; sales tax; credit card sales; and auditing.

You can work at home as a professional bookkeeper and make only necessary visits to your client's place of work.

Training

Bookkeepers must be trained in accounting procedures. You can take courses offered at community colleges or complete a home study program. Bookkeepers must know basic math skills and be able to organize. There is no license required to work as a bookkeeper.

For more information contact

At Home Professions
2001 Lowe Street
Fort Collins, CO 80525-3474
970-282-6320
Home study bookkeeping course

National Career Institute
2021 West Montrose Avenue
Chicago, IL 60618
Home study bookkeeping course

· BOOK READER ·

Career Description

A book reader is a person who is hired by publishers to read unpublished manuscripts and evaluate them.

Career Opportunities

Believe it or not, you can be paid to read books. When a writer writes a book, he or she usually sends it to a publisher. The publisher then reads the book and determines whether or not to buy and publish the book. Quite often, publishers have an overload of unread manuscripts. The publishers hire freelance readers to read the manuscripts and give an honest opinion and evaluation of the work.

To get this kind of work, write letters to publishers letting them know that you are a professional book reader and will provide them with an honest evaluation of their manuscripts.

Most book readers work from home and charge publishers a per-book reading rate. Books are read by the reader as quickly as possible and returned with a written evaluation report. The report should point out any problems with the manuscript and should have a section for the reader's review. Send your introductory letter with a few sample reports to acquisitions editors at publishing houses, and to literary agents as well.

Recommended Reading

The Writer's Guide to Book Editors, Publishers, and Literary Agents, Jeff Herman, Prima Publishing, updated yearly—List of publishers and agents to contact

The Writer's Market, Writer's Digest Books, F&W Publications, updated yearly

· BUSINESS BROKER ·

Career Description

A business broker is a professional who works as an agent between buyers and sellers of businesses.

Career Opportunities

Businesses of all types are on the market for sale, from small retail stores to large companies. Business brokers specialize in matching up buyers and sellers of these businesses and receive a commission (about 10 percent of the total sale) once the transaction is complete.

Business brokers are able to determine the value of a business. The value of a business is generally based upon the following:

Profits—How much money does the business gross and net each year?

Establishment—How many years has the business been established?

Location—If it is a retail business, is the location good? Is there foot traffic? Is there adequate parking?

Assets—What are the assets of the business and what are they worth? Company vehicles, computers and inventory are a few examples.

Growth—How fast has the company expanded? What is the future outlook for the growth of this business?

Customer database—Does the company have a database of loyal customers?

These are some of the factors that business brokers use to determine the value and asking price of a business.

Business brokers advertise businesses for sale and negotiate the best deals for their clients. Brokers usually specialize in certain types of businesses, such as car washes or restaurants.

Training

In some states, business brokers are required to have a real estate license. Check with your State Board of Realtors to find out what is required in your area. Many business brokers start off as apprentices for established brokers to learn the business. Also, see entry for Real Estate Agent.

For more information contact

Entrepreneur Magazines
Small Business Resource Catalog
638 Lindero Canyon Road #302
Agoura Hills, CA 91301
1-800-421-2300
Training manual for business brokers—ask for catalog

Recommended Reading

Buying and Selling a Small Business, Small Business Administration, Superintendent of Documents, U.S. Government Printing Office, Washington, D.C. 20402

· CAKE DECORATOR · ·

Career Description

A cake decorator is a person who bakes and decorates beautiful specialty cakes for clients.

Career Opportunities

Cake decorators bake, decorate and sell cakes to clients for special occasions. Specialty cakes are most often bought by clients who are celebrating weddings, anniversaries, birthdays and other special occasions. Specialty cakes are also popular around holidays such as Thanksgiving, Christmas, Chanukah, Valentine's Day, St. Patrick's Day and Easter.

Cake decorators bake their own cakes using shaped molds or buy plain cakes from bakeries. The cakes are then artistically decorated with icing, fancy borders, flowers and other decorations made with different colored cake icing. Wedding cakes are a cake decorator's biggest selling item. Elaborate cakes are ordered by clients in advance. The cake decorator helps clients choose styles, colors and cake flavors. These sometimes spectacular cakes usually consist of several different cake layers which are stacked on top of one another using columns and cardboard support discs.

Cake decorators can work from home, or on a freelance basis with local bakeries. Cake decorators are skilled in the art of decorating cakes and must know how to use special tools like the tips that are used to dispense icing into beautiful designs such as flowers, leaves, writing, swirls and borders.

Training

Cake decorators are not required to have any formal training or hold any special certificates. Cake decorators who bake at home may be required in some states to have a food preparation license. Cake decorating can be learned by reading books on the subject and practicing. Some community colleges and craft stores offer cake decorating classes. Cake decorating equipment can be purchased at most cooking supply shops, craft supply stores and some party supply shops. Practice is important and the only way to develop professional skills as a decorator.

For more information contact

Cake Decorating Institute
P.O. Box 13986
Palm Desert, CA 92255
1-800-941-2284

Home-study cake decorating and ice sculpting training programs

Wilton Enterprises
P.O. Box 1604
Woodridge, IL 60517-0750
1-800-942-8881
Cake decorating classes, cake decorating kits, pans, decorating tips, how-to books and other supplies

Recommended Reading

The Cake Decorator's Bible, Angela Nilsen and Sarah Maxwell, Smithmark Publishers, 1996

· CALLIGRAPHER ·

Career Description

A calligrapher is a person who handwrites in a highly decorative manner in beautiful penmanship.

Career Opportunities

Calligraphers are hired on a freelance basis to handwrite letters, certificates, invitations and other important documents that call for aesthetic lettering.

Calligraphers work with ink pens with special nibs or tips. These special calligraphy pen tips come in different widths, and the pens can be filled with a wide variety of colored ink cartridges. Calligraphy supplies can be purchased at art supply stores.

Calligraphers most often use old-fashioned lettering techniques. Most calligraphers are able to produce several different alphabet styles that their clients can choose from.

Calligraphy can be done from home and can be a great part-time career. Individuals who need invitations written for weddings, parties and other formal occasions hire calligraphers to do the handwriting. Universities, schools and businesses also hire calligraphers to handwrite the names of graduates and employees on diplomas and certificates.

Training

There is no formal training required to become a calligrapher. Calligraphers usually learn their trade by taking classes in calligraphy, which are available through most community colleges and some art programs. Other calligraphers learn by reading books on the subject and then practicing their art. There are many books and workbooks about calligraphy, which are available at bookstores, libraries and art supply stores. No matter how you learn calligraphy, practice is necessary to perfect your skills.

Recommended Reading

Calligraphy School: A Step-by-Step Guide to the Fine Art of Lettering, Gaynor Goffe and Anna Ravenscroft, Reader's Digest Association, Inc., 1994

The Complete Guide to Calligraphy, Judy Martin, Chartwell Books, Inc., 1993

· CAMP COUNSELOR ·

Career Description

A camp counselor is a person who supervises, plans and coordinates children's activities at camp.

Career Opportunities

Camp counseling is seasonal work, usually during the summer and spring seasons. There are thousands of camps across the country that employ seasonal counselors.

Counselors are usually assigned a group of children for which they are responsible. Counselors may organize and supervise recreational activities such as hiking, crafts, swimming, dancing, horseback riding, storytelling and games. At overnight camps, counselors must keep an eye out for mischief and make sure that the children go to sleep.

Most camps are located in mountainous or lake areas. Camp counselors must enjoy working outdoors and with children. Each campground has different hiring procedures for seasonal counselors. Call campgrounds in your area to find out what qualifications are required.

Training

There is no formal training necessary to become a camp counselor, although most counselors are required to know emergency first aid procedures. Counselors should also know how to manage groups of children and how to organize activities.

For more information contact

Office of Information
Forest Service, Department of Agriculture
Room 3238, South Building
Washington, DC 20250
General information and listing of camping facilities in our national forests

Recommended Reading

Woodall's Campground Management, Woodall Publishing Company, 28167 North Keith Drive, Lake Forest, IL 60045-4528—Monthly tabloid covering campground management and operation

THE 101 BEST FREELANCE CAREERS

· CANDLE MAKER ·

Career Description

A candle maker is a person who handcrafts candles from wax.

Career Opportunities

Candles have been used by man as a source of light for thousands of years. Today candles are still used as a light source, but usually for aesthetic purposes such as mood lighting and decoration.

Candles come in all shapes and sizes, from the elaborately carved and colored to plain and simple designs. Candles can be molded into many shapes using candle molds, such as round, square, flowers, animals, and other figures. Hot wax can also be poured into sealed canisters or tins. Natural beeswax candles can be made by wrapping sheets of plain or colored beeswax around a wick for stunning, natural looking candles. Other candle makers dip candles with several different layers of colored wax and then carve designs into the candles to create a multicolored effect. Some candle makers add trinkets, sand, glitter, flowers and other decorative things to the wax of their candles to create interesting textures. Scent—such as vanilla, orange, strawberry, rose, jasmine and pine—can be added to candles to create a sweet-smelling environment as your candles burn.

Most candle makers work at home or out of their workshops. Finished candles can be sold to retail stores, boutiques, gift shops, candle shops, to individuals or by mail order.

Training

There is no training required to become a candle maker. Candle making requires practice to produce aesthetic candles that will sell. There are many how-to books available about candle making, which can be bought from bookstores, craft stores and through candle-making suppliers.

For more information contact

General Wax and Candle Company
P.O. Box 9398
North Hollywood, CA 91609
(818) 765-5800
Beeswax, molds, books and candle-making supplies

Pourette
P.O. Box 17056
Seattle, WA 98107
1-800-888-9425
Candle-making supplies, molds, colors, scents, how-to books
and waxes

• CANDY AND CONFECTION MAKER •

Career Description
A candy maker is a person who makes, designs and sells
candy. Candy makers usually follow recipes and sometimes develop their own. This is a great career if you want to work at
home and enjoy being in the kitchen.

Career Opportunities
Candy can be made in the kitchen and then sold to markets,
by mail order, to retail shops and many other outlets. Some of
the most popular candies are fudge, hard candy, lollipops, taffy,
truffles, caramels and mints.
Many candy makers specialize in chocolates. Chocolates can
be filled with cream fillings, cherries, nuts and caramels. These
chocolates are then dipped in light or dark chocolate and decorated with swirls and other designs made of white chocolate.
A woman in Los Angeles developed her own line of all-natural

cough drops using a hard candy recipe and adding lemon oil and honey for a soothing, sore throat lozenge.

Packaging is important. Candy should be either wrapped in cellophane or packaged in boxes. You'll want to ensure that your candy is fresh if you're going to sell it. Many candy makers have small labels made up with their name, phone number and ingredients, which they attach to their candy so that customers can easily reorder. Candy packaging supplies such as boxes, paper cups and wrappers are available from candy-making suppliers, craft stores and some specialty cooking shops.

There are many cookbooks available on the subject of candy making, which can be found in bookstores and some cooking supply shops.

Training

There is no training or education required to become a candy maker. You will need to practice your recipes until perfect. Your city or state may require you to have a food preparation license to operate this type of business.

For more information contact

Lorann Oils
4518 Aurelius Road
P.O. Box 22009
Lansing, MI 48909-2009
1-800-248-1302
Candy-making supplies and recipes

Wilton Enterprises
P.O. Box 1604
Woodridge, IL 60517-0750
1-800-942-8881
Candy-making supplies

Recommended Reading

Candy Cookbook, Mildred Brand, Ideals Publishing Corporation

Candy Industry, Advanstar Communications, Inc., 7500 Old Oak Blvd., Cleveland, OH 44130, (216) 891-2612—Monthly magazine for candy and confectionery makers

Candymaking, Ruth A. Kendrick & Pauline H. Atkinsin, HP Books, 1987

· CHAUFFEUR ·

Career Description

A chauffeur is a person hired to drive automobiles for others. The word "chauffeur" comes from the French verb *chauffer*, which means "to heat." Early-model automobiles were powered by steam and the drivers had to "stoke" or add fuel to the furnace that heated the water. Chauffeuring has come a long way since then and today chauffeurs are only required to drive automobiles for their clients.

Career Opportunities

Chauffeurs usually work freelance for their clients and drive the client's car. Chauffeurs usually work for celebrities, executives and wealthy families. Some chauffeurs wear uniforms, the traditional black cap and coat.

Chauffeurs must have a clean driving record and should be familiar with car maintenance and road maps. Some chauffeurs also maintain and clean the automobiles of their clients.

Chauffeurs may also work freelance for limousine services. Limousine drivers are responsible for driving executives, celebrities, high-profile clients and others who rent limousine services.

Some limousine drivers own their own limousines and rent them out.

Training

There is no training required to become a chauffeur. A driver's license is necessary for this type of work and chauffeurs must have a clean driving record. Chauffeurs need to be familiar with the streets and freeway systems in their area. Chauffeurs should have good references. A course in auto maintenance is recommended for chauffeurs to learn simple car repairs such as changing tires, changing oil, checking and replacing fluids and how to jump-start a car. Chauffeurs may also want to learn simple auto detailing techniques such as washing, waxing, polishing and caring for car interiors.

For more information contact

National Limousine Driver's Association
Attn: Phillip Wockner
747 Oxford Avenue
Marina Del Rey, CA 90292-54302
1-800-547-8442
Chauffeur training programs

Recommended Reading

All About Your Car, David Kline and Jamie Robertson, Dimi Press, 1996

Chilton's Auto Repair Manual, Chilton, annual publication about auto repair

What's Wrong With My Car?, Bob Cerullo, Penguin Books, 1993

· CHIMNEY INSPECTOR ·

Career Description

A chimney inspector is an individual who inspects chimneys for safety. Unlike the chimney sweep, who only cleans the chimney, the inspector uses internal video cameras to detect cracks, which can make a chimney unsafe to use. Inspectors also conduct smoke tests, a procedure for detecting internal chimney cracks by using smoke bombs and looking for smoke escapage through chimney walls.

Career Opportunities

No homeowner should consider his or her chimney safe without first having a thorough chimney inspection. Rain, soot buildup, earthquakes and old age can be a few causes of chimney erosion and damage.

In the past, chimney inspections were done by using a flashlight and mirror, but today, internal video cameras and pressurized smoke tests are used. Inspectors provide a written report of their findings and usually provide a copy of the videotaped inspections. Their clients include the following:

Homeowners—Homeowners and realtors often hire chimney inspectors to inspect chimneys of homes before they are bought and sold.

Insurance companies—Insurance companies often hire inspectors to evaluate the condition of chimneys to verify work needed.

Home inspectors—Home inspectors often refer clients to chimney inspectors to conduct thorough inspections of the chimney.

General contractors—General contractors hire chimney inspectors to evaluate work needed on their clients' chimneys.

Training

There is no license required to perform chimney inspections. An inspector must know how to operate chimney cameras and how to conduct smoke tests. There is information available to learn this simple technology.

For more information contact

Fireplace Freddie
Department of Training
3033 Angus Street
Los Angeles, CA 90039
Information on starting a chimney inspection business

· CLOCK REPAIRER ·

Career Description

A clock repairer is a skilled craftsman who fixes broken clocks. There are many types of clocks and many things can go wrong with them. A clock repairer knows how to diagnose and remedy problems. Clock repairs can be as simple as giving the clock a cleaning, or may require more complicated procedures such as replacing gears or resetting the springs.

Career Opportunities

Clock repairer—As long as clocks exist, there will be a need for clock repairers. Most clock repairers have their own shops and some work from their home workshops. Clock repairing is a great career for people who love tinkering with mechanical parts. Clock repairers may be hired to clean clocks, wind springs, replace parts, reset gears, repair chimes and lubricate parts.
Watch repairers—Clock repairers sometimes repair watches. The mechanics of watches are much smaller than clocks and need a skilled craftsman with a steady hand and delicate touch to prop-

erly repair them. Watch repairers must understand how watches operate and how to use the appropriate tools.

Clock making—There are kits available to make popular clocks such as grandfather and mantel clocks. Clocks made from kits can be assembled by clock makers and sold for retail prices, earning the maker hundreds, even thousands, of dollars in profit.

Training

Clock work takes a lot of skill and expertise. Clock repairers must be knowledgeable about all types of clocks, antique and modern, and understand how each works. Most clock repairers start as apprentices or attend a clock-repairing school to learn the trade. Many clock repairers have their own shops, while others work at home.

For more information contact

Clock Repair Center
33 Boyd Drive
Westbury, NY 11590
Clock repair parts, tools, supplies and books—send $5.95 for 190-page catalog

Emperor Clock Company
Emperor Industrial Park
P.O. Box 1089
Fairhope, AL 36533-1089
(334) 928-2316
Clock-making kits and clock-repair classes

hr: MAGAZINE
1012 Broadway
Dunedin, FL 34698

1-877-497-4557
Magazine about fine watches and unique timepieces

The Joseph Bulova School
40-24 62nd Street
Woodside, NY 11377
Watch-making and -repair training

Recommended reading
The Clock Repairer's Handbook, Laurie Penman, Arco Publishing, 1985

Practical Clock Repairing, Donald de Carle, Wehman Brothers, 1979

· COLLECTION AGENT ·

Career Description
A collection agent is a person hired by businesses and other organizations to collect past-due bills and accounts receivable from customers.

Career Opportunities
Many companies have accounts receivable for which they have not been able to collect payment on. For example, a plumbing company may have a payment account with a customer. Say the customer falls behind on his or her payments. The plumbing company may have tried to collect the money unsuccessfully, or they just might not have time to check up on all of their overdue accounts. This is where you can step in as a freelance collection agent.

Approach small- to medium-sized service companies (most large companies have their own internal collection departments) and tell them that you are a freelance collection agent. Work out an agreement with them that you will collect their unpaid accounts for 25 to 50 percent of the money collected. The company will probably hire you immediately, as they have nothing to lose and only the collected amount to gain!

This is a great business to operate from home. Just get permission to bring the uncollected account information to your home or make copies of the paperwork and bring that home with you.

How to Collect

1. Set up a post office box so that customers can mail their payments to you. Make sure that the customer makes out all payments to the name of the company you will be working for.

2. Start off with a pleasant phone call to the customer and remind him or her that the payment is overdue. You may find that the customer just forgot about the bill. Make notes of when you called each customer and what arrangements were made.

3. Have the customer send his or her payment to your post office box. You may be able to collect the whole payment, or you can work out a payment schedule with the customer.

4. If your pleasant phone calls don't work, work with the owner of the company to get permission to design a collection bill that would be appropriate. Bills that say things like the following seem to work well: "You have failed to pay the remaining balance of $450.00 on your account with JB Plumbing. Please handle this immediately to avoid further action."

Training

There is no license required to become a collection agent. There are computer software programs available to help collection agents organize and manage accounts.

For more information contact

The American Collectors Association
P.O. Box 39106
Minneapolis, MN 55439-0106
(612) 926-6547
Information and publications about collecting

Recommended Reading

Collection Techniques for a Small Business, Gini Graham Scott and John J. Harrison, Oasis Press, 1994—A complete guide for collecting with sample forms included

· COMMERCIAL ACTOR ·

Career Description

A commercial actor is a person who acts or is featured in a television or radio advertisement for services or products.

Career Opportunities

How would you like to be in a television commercial? There are many opportunities for all types and ages of people to break into commercial acting. Corporate America uses new talent on a daily basis to promote their products and image.

Commercial actors usually begin their careers by learning to apply audition techniques such as reading a script. They then either sign up with a talent agent or go directly to auditions and start auditioning for parts.

Besides television and radio commercials, actors are often hired to act in corporate industrial films, public service announcements and do voiceovers. Many actors begin their careers in commercials, which can lead to working on motion pictures and television series.

Training

There is no formal training required to become a commercial actor. Commerical actors must be able to memorize and deliver their lines naturally. This skill can be learned easily and practiced to perfection in the privacy of your own home. There are many acting schools and books available on the subject.

For more information contact:

Kathy Smith Casting
13527 Ventura Blvd.
Sherman Oaks, CA 91423
(818) 907-1717
Books, tapes and training materials to learn how to break into the business of commercial acting

· COMMUNITY COLLEGE INSTRUCTOR ·

Career Description

A community college instructor is a person who teaches extracurricular and continued education classes to students.

Career Opportunities

Community colleges offer a wide variety of community services courses. These courses are offered to the public by the college and are usually taught by freelance instructors. Many people take these short courses to meet new friends, learn a new hobby or skill or just to get out of the house. Most of the courses offered are taught on weeknights or weekends and only last a few hours.

You can become a course instructor and make a good living at it. Courses cost between $30 to $150 and cover subjects like art, health, language, self-defense, cooking, crafting, finances, fashion and personal growth.

The college mails out a catalog of courses and people call to sign up. The college then takes a percentage of the course fee and the rest is given to the instructor as his or her pay. Sometimes the instructor is paid an additional fee by students when they arrive at the door, to cover the costs of materials to be used during the class. This fee can range from $5.00 to $30.00 depending upon what materials will be used.

In order to teach a class, you must know how to do something of interest. I have seen courses taught on the art of flirting, candy making, floral arranging, résumé writing, self-defense, calligraphy, quilting, and a number of other easy-to-teach subjects. Figure out what you can teach others to do in a short time and how to break it up into graduated levels that others can understand. For example, if you teach a class on how to make quilts and your class is broken up over two Saturday afternoons, you might spend the first hour going over the history of quilt making, then spend the rest of that first class teaching the students how to piece together fabric, and then have them work on it at home during the week. Then, the next week, you would spend helping the students put together their final projects.

Call your local community college and request their current catalog and see what they offer. Then call them back and tell them you're interested in teaching a course.

Training
The training required for a course instructor varies with each subject.

· COMPUTER TUTOR ·

Career Description

A computer tutor is a person who teaches others how to use computers or software programs.

Career Opportunities

In today's computerized world, one must know how to operate computers and computer programs to survive. Computer tutors must know how to operate computer systems and be able to teach others on graduated levels.

Tutors are frequently hired by businesses who want to teach their employees to operate new systems. Many businesses will hire a tutor for a day to hold a company class on a new system.

Tutors are hired by individuals when they've just purchased a new computer or software program. Often the tutor will come to the client's home, unpack the computer, load in the software and teach the client the basics of operating the system.

There is also plenty of room for computer consultants. Consultants usually work for businesses and may help clients choose new computer systems and programs, develop efficient data entry programs and set up computer networking systems.

Training

There is no required certificate or license to become a computer tutor. Tutors must know how to operate the systems and programs that they will be teaching to others.

Recommended Reading

How to Be a Successful Computer Consultant, Alan R. Simon, McGraw-Hill, 1994

· CONSULTANT ·

Career Description

A consultant is a person who is hired to solve problems for others by using knowledge, skill, education and experience.

Career Opportunities

There are many career opportunities available to consultants in all fields. In order to be a consultant, you must be an expert on the subject on which you are consulting. There are thousands of fields in which a consultant might work, so we'll only be looking at a few diverse examples to give you a taste of the unlimited possibilities.

The key to making it as a consultant is to have the ability to solve problems for others quickly and efficiently. A good consultant can analyze the circumstances and skillfully solve problems. Remember, if the problem were an easy one to solve, your client would not have hired you.

We'll look at a few examples of how ordinary skills can be turned into creative consulting work.

Computer consultant—Bill has a background in computers. He works freelance as a consultant for large corporations helping them to set up new computer systems. He would be called a computer consultant.

Small business consultant—Fred owns a small heating and air-conditioning company which he started and has been operating for twenty years. During his slow seasons, he offers his knowledge and expertise to people who are just getting started in the field. He helps other small businesses grow by consulting them. He would be called a small business consultant.

Security consultant—John is a retired police officer from the fraud division. He now works consulting large corporations on internal security measures. He would be called a security consultant.

Entertainment consultant—Jenny is a housewife who is married to a doctor. Over the years she has planned many parties and dinners to entertain her husband's colleagues and associates. Jenny knows how to plan great parties and offers her services to others and plans their parties. She would be called a party planning consultant.

Buying consultant—Maria worked for a shoe store as a buyer. She had a knack for picking styles that sold well for her store. Being an expert in the shoe business, she began consulting other shoe stores on the styles they should buy. She would be called a buying consultant.

Training

The training a consultant needs depends on what he or she will be consulting others about.

Recommended Reading

Getting into the Consulting Business, Steve Kahn, Longmeadow Press, 1987

How to Start and Run a Successful Consulting Business, Gregory Kishel and Patricia Kishel, John Wiley & Sons, 1996

· CORPORATE INVESTIGATOR ·

Career Description

A corporate investigator is an individual hired on a freelance basis by a corporation to conduct internal investigations. The investigator is hired to find facts, uncover the source of problems and ensure the safety of the corporation. This type of investigator is almost always working undercover and poses as a regular em-

THE 101 BEST FREELANCE CAREERS

ployee. This career requires no law enforcement background. The duties and assignments a corporate investigator my receive are widely varied.

Career Opportunities

Here are a few of the many possibilities:

Pre-employment investigations—An agent may be hired by a company to conduct background searches on potential employees. This usually entails confirming and extracting information to determine the accuracy of a person's reported background. This information could include searching public records for criminal convictions, checking with previous employers, verifying education and checking references.

Undercover agent—This type of investigator infiltrates specific target groups inside or outside the company and gains access to illegal activity and breaches of security. Many large corporations hire undercover agents who pose as regular employees. A few of the reasons you might be hired would be to find employee drug use and/or sale, theft of company property, trade-secret theft and other illegal activity. The agent gains the trust of suspects and keeps notes on their activity. He then writes and submits reports on his findings. An added bonus to this particular field is that the agent is paid a double salary for his or her work, the agent salary and the employee "cover" salary.

Electronic countermeasures—An investigator may be hired by a corporation to conduct searches and or set up hidden microphones, closed-circuit TV, tracking and monitoring equipment, and phone taps.

Undercover consumer—An investigator may be hired by hotels, restaurants, retail chain stores and even amusement parks to conduct service and safety reports. The investigator is hired by the company to pose as an ordinary customer and make a written report on things such as cleanliness, safety and employee attitude.

Training

It is not necessary to be a licensed private investigator to start the above careers. Training for these careers is available and there are many books on the subject of conducting investigations and undercover work.

For more information contact

American Innovations, Inc.
119 Rockland Center, Suite 315
Nanuet, NY 10954
Countersurveillance equipment by mail order, write for catalog

American Society of Industrial Security
1655 North Fort Myer Drive, Suite #1200
Arlington, VA 22209-3198
Educational training courses, information and industry publications for security professionals

Nick Harris Detective Academy
16917 Enadia Way
Van Nuys, CA 91406
1-800-642-5427
Corporate investigations training program

Bare Associates International Restaurant and Hotel Services
(703) 591-9870
http://www.rhscorp.com
Nationwide job placement and training for freelance under-cover consumers or "mystery shoppers" for restaurants, hotels, retail stores, health clubs and golf courses

West Coast Detective Academy
5113 Lankershim Blvd.

North Hollywood, CA 91601
1-800-752-5555
Investigator training program

Recommended Reading
Business Intelligence Investigations, Ralph Thomas, Thomas Publications, 1991

Check It Out: The Ultimate Guide to Background Investigations, Edmund G. Pankau, Thomas Publication, 1991

The Guide to Professional Mystery Shopping, LS Enterprise, P.O. Box 9535-1000, New Haven, CT 06534—A complete training and job resourse manual for mystery shoppers

Security Consulting, Charles A. Sennewald, Butterworths, 1989

Security Management Bulletin, Bureau of Business Practice, 24 Rope Ferry Road, Waterford, CT 06386—Semi-monthly newsletter for the security industry

· COURT REPORTER ·

Career Description
A court reporter is a stenographer who records and transcribes an official, verbatim, written record of the legal proceedings in a court of law.

Career Opportunities
Court reporters produce official transcripts of court proceedings, which may include testimonies of witnesses, judges' comments, cross-examinations of attorneys and all other

communication that takes place while court is in session. The transcripts that the reporter produces are verbatim accounts of the spoken words and become the legal records of cases. Most court reporters today use computers to create transcripts, while some still use stenotype machines. Court reporters must listen intently and write approximately 72,000 words per day (in shorthand of course!)

These days, court reporters have many fields in which they can make money using their skills.

Official reporters—Official reporters are court reporters who work in courtrooms. Many official reporters work full-time on salary for courts and government agencies. They may receive additional pay for transcription work done after hours, on nights and weekends to meet deadlines.

Freelance reporters—Freelance reporters work for themselves and take short-term assignments from clients. Freelance reporters often take depositions, which are testimonies taken from witnesses by attorneys to use as evidence in cases. The freelance reporter travels to the location of the deposition. Freelance reporters may also transcribe and record arbitrations which take place out of the courtroom at places such as hotels, law offices, crime scenes, accident sites and many other places at which an official record is needed. Reporters may also be hired by corporations to take meeting notes, by law enforcement agencies to write reports and by lawyers to do legal transcription and to take notes and make transcriptions at meetings.

Real-time captioners—Real-time captioners use their court reporting skills to produce captions of live television programs, news events, sporting events and other television programs for the hearing impaired audience. The spoken words are taken down by the reporter on a computerized stenotype and transmitted with the broadcasting signal to the viewer's television screen. This service enables people with impaired hearing to understand the programs they watch.

Training

Court reporters must be proficient in the English language, be able to meet deadlines, use computers, be knowledgeable about courtroom proceedings, be computer literate and be technically trained as a court reporter. Some states require court reporters to be state certified, while others do not. Contact your state's regulatory agency to find out what is required. Court reporting training programs are available through trade schools and some community colleges. Every state has several court reporting training programs available. Look in the yellow pages under "Vocational Schools" or "Court Reporting." Training programs usually take two to four years to complete.

For more information contact

National Court Reporters Association
8224 Old Courthouse Road
Vienna, VA 22182-3808
1-800-272-6272
Membership organization that provides career information, seminars, court reporting products and a support network for reporters, publishers of *The Journal of Court Reporting*

· CREDIT REPAIR CONSULTANT ·

Career Description

A credit repair consultant is a person who helps others clean up their bad credit with credit bureaus and helps them to establish a good credit record.

Career Opportunities

Bad credit is something that many people are all too familiar with. Department stores, credit card companies, gas stations, utility companies, banks, and many other organizations that offer lines of credit, report credit records to credit bureaus. A late payment on a bill, bankruptcies, liens and even applying for too many credit cards can make serious dents in a person's credit rating, which then makes it nearly impossible to obtain loans and other lines of credit.

Credit repair consultants work with clients to help them clean up some or all of their negative credit records. A consultant may help clients write letters of explanation and letters of dispute to credit reporting bureaus regarding negative and/or false reports, which may result in removal of the report from the record. Consultants also help their clients establish good credit records by doing such things as applying for secured credit cards and making timely payments, and may also consult them on how to look good to banks and loan officers.

Credit repair consultants are hired by individuals and businesses looking to improve their credit ratings.

Training

There is no formal training or licensing required to become a credit repair consultant. Consultants should understand credit cards, loans and how credit bureaus work. There are some good books about credit repair available in bookstores and libraries.

For more information contact

Credit & Debt Consultant Institute, Inc.
Institute Building
P.O. Box 145087
Coral Gables, FL 33114-5087
(305) 661-0606
Training programs for credit repair consultants

Recommended Reading
   The Credit Repair Kit, John Ventura, Dearborn Financial Publishing, Inc., 1996

   The E-Z Legal Guide to Credit Repair, E-Z Legal Forms, Inc., 1995
An excellent and simple book on how to repair credit, with legal forms and sample letters included

· DESKTOP PUBLISHER ·

Career Description
   A desktop publisher is a person who publishes documents using a personal computer, page layout software and laser printer.

Career Opportunities
   Personal computers and publishing programs allow even beginners to produce professional work at a fraction of the cost of a commercial publisher. A desktop publisher may perform a wide variety of tasks for clients, such as writing, editing, planning and design. A desktop publisher creates documents for clients. Clients may include businesses, organizations, stores, clubs and individuals.
   Most desktop publishers work freelance in their home office. There are software programs available to create brochures, newsletters and clip art.
   There are many opportunities for desktop publishers. A few examples of work that a publisher might be hired to do are advertisements, business cards, letterhead, greeting cards, business forms, reports, newsletters, charts, graphs and even books.

Training
   There is no license required to become a desktop publisher. Most publishers start by working with a desktop publishing pro-

gram, of which there are many. There are also style books and books about desktop publishing available at bookstores and libraries. Computer stores sell software for desktop publishers, such as clip art libraries, brochure layouts and newsletter layouts. It is necessary to own a good computer and laser printer.

· DIETITIAN ·

Career Description

A dietitian is a highly qualified professional recognized as an expert on food and nutrition.

Eating healthy plays a vital part in the lives of many people today. People are now more than ever focusing on nutrition to attain good health. People are eager to learn more about good nutrition and how they can change their eating habits. The field of dietetics is rapidly expanding and provides many career opportunities.

Career Opportunities

Clinical dietitians work in hospitals, nursing homes and medical offices. They work with the medical team to help patients recover through good nutrition. Dietitians can also work individually with patients to educate them about the best nutritional program for them.

Management dietitians work with schools, cafeterias and restaurants to plan healthy menus. They may also manage personnel, budgeting and purchasing for their department.

Research dietitians work with government agencies, food manufacturers and at universities. They conduct experiments and clinical trials to find answers to nutritional problems and search for alternative foods for those with allergies or special nutritional requirements. They may also set dietary recommendations for the public.

Consultant dietitians work freelance for health care facilities, consulting patients on diet-related health issues. Some consultants have their own private practice where they offer advice on weight loss and cholesterol reduction and educate their patients about what to eat to help them attain their goals.

Business dietitians work in food-related industries such as manufacturing. They help with product development, sales, advertising, public relations, purchasing and in many other areas that assist the company in satisfying the consumer's interest in nutrition.

Training

To become a registered dietitian you will need training. You may either enroll in an American Dietetic Association–accredited coordinated program at a community, city or state college, which is a bachelor's or master's degree program that combines classroom and supervised practical experience. You may also enroll in an American Dietetic Association–approved bachelor's program at a community, city or state college and then complete an approved dietetic internship. After you have completed either of the above requirements, you then qualify to take the registration examination for dietitians. When you pass, you are then considered a qualified expert on food and nutrition.

For more information contact

The American Dietetic Association
216 West Jackson Blvd.
Chicago, IL 60606-6995
1-800-877-1600
Information about the field of dietetics, career opportunities and accredited training programs

· DIVER ·

Career Description

A commercial diver is a person who dives or performs work underwater professionally. There are many exciting and challenging jobs and opportunities available for divers. Divers primarily work in the ocean, but sometimes lakes.

Career Opportunities

Salvage diver—A salvage diver is a person who searches for items underwater. You may be hired to search for planes, shipwrecks, personal items and anything else that has become lost in the water. Many salvage divers work for themselves looking for items of value.

Inspection—An inspection diver works on underwater job sites both inland and offshore. Steel and other construction materials are prone to deterioration from a wide range of causes. A diver may be hired to inspect underwater structures and machinery for corrosion, breakdowns and regular maintenance checks. The diver may visually inspect, take still photographs, videos and conduct tests to ensure structural safety.

Welder—Divers trained in underwater welding are in constant demand. The work involves welding and repairing steel structures underwater. When welding is called for on a job site, only qualified and trained welders may be hired.

Seafood—Divers often work freelance diving for seafood such as abalone, crabs, lobsters, oysters, sea urchins, scallops and clams.

Search and rescue—Divers are hired frequently by the police department to search for missing persons. Divers are also hired to look for evidence and bodies at underwater homicide scenes.

Diving journalists and underwater photographers—Some divers write for diving magazines, books and even screenplays about their underwater adventures. Writers must have good writing skills. Underwater photographers bring the underwater world to the surface with photos and film. They must be trained to use special cameras and equipment. They sell their work to all areas of the media for publication.

Training

To work as a commercial diver you must complete a training program and obtain a license. Divers must be in good physical condition. Diving is a potentially hazardous occupation and involves some risk.

For more information contact

Association of Commercial Diving Educators (ACDE)
P.O. Box 30100
Flagstaff, AZ 86003-0100
(520) 527-1055
List of accredited diving schools, books and information about commercial diving careers

College of Oceaneering
272 South Fries Avenue
Wilmington, CA 90744
1-800-432-3483
Commercial diving training programs

Diver's Academy of the Eastern Seaboard
2500 South Broadway
Camden, NJ 08104
1-800-238-3483
Commercial diving training programs

Recommended Reading

Treasure Diver, Double Eagle Publishing, 31970 Yucaipa Blvd., Yucaipa, CA 92399, (909) 794-4612—Bimonthly magazine for treasure divers

· DOLL DOCTOR ·

Career Description

A doll doctor or repairer is a person who repairs delicate antique and broken dolls. Doll doctors operate doll hospitals or workshops and restore their little patients as closely as possible to their original condition.

Career Opportunities

Dolls, particularly older models and antiques, are delicate and often need to be repaired due to old age and use. Dolls are cherished by many people, from serious collectors to dreamy-eyed little girls.

A doll hospital provides specialized care for broken dolls and can also repair the broken heart of the doll's owner.

Doll heads and limbs are made from many different materials, such as wood, metal, rubber, china, bisque and, of course, plastic, all of which can be repaired using different techniques. Doll bodies are made of cloth, leather, wood and china. Sometimes the joints need to be repaired or the body restuffed. Doll repairing materials such as plaster, tools and paint can be purchased at most large craft supply stores. Patterns for making new doll clothes can be purchased at fabric supply stores.

Doll repairing takes a delicate and artistic touch.

Training

There is no formal training or licensing required to repair dolls or to open a doll hospital. Read books about doll repair and practice repairs before you attempt to work on your first client's cherished doll.

Recommended Reading
Doll Repair, Evelyn Gaylin, 1974

Dolls, Collector Communications Corporation, 170 Fifth Avenue, New York, NY 10010-5911, (212) 989-8700—Magazine published ten times a year covering doll collecting, restoration and collections

How to Mend China and Bric-a-brac, Paul St.-Gaudens and Arthur R. Jackson, Charles T. Branford Company, 1953

How to Repair and Dress Old Dolls, Audrey Johnson, Charles T. Branford Company, 1967

· DRESSMAKER ·

Career Description
A professional dressmaker designs and creates dresses and clothing for clients. Dressmakers may also design special creations for boutiques and can do alterations.

Career Opportunities
Sewing used to be a skill that was passed down from mothers to daughters. These days, our world is full of mass-manufactured garments and the art of sewing has nearly become lost. There is a great demand for skilled seamstresses who can design and create clothing. Dressmaking is a wonderful opportunity to use your creativity to make a living. The best dressmakers know how to sew garments and must own a sewing machine. It is important

to know your fabrics and to have good taste in patterns, designs and colors.

Clothing Design—A dressmaker can create and sell dresses and clothing. These garments can be specially made for individuals or for boutiques and stores. One woman makes her living designing replicas of antique clothing and uses old patterns for ideas. Another woman makes spectacular evening gowns for a very upscale boutique in her neighborhood. Another woman started making women's swimwear in her garage workshop; just two years later, her creative bathing suits can be found in department stores all over the country.

Alterations—A good seamstress can always get work doing clothing alterations. Alterations may include shortening or letting out hems, mending tears, taking in clothing that is too large or updating clothing. Most alterers work freelance in their own shops or are referred by stores and dry cleaners.

Repair—A skilled seamstress can repair almost anything made of fabric. Some items that you might repair are drapery, lace, vintage clothing, linens, quilts and upholstery. Some seamstresses are trained in the specialized art of invisible reweaving. Reweaving techniques can be used to repair tears, moth holes and cigarette burns.

Home Furnishings and accessories—You can sew and sell fabulous home furnishings and make huge profits. Some of the items that an experienced seamstress can create are bedspreads, sheets, pillows, tablecloths, napkins, slipcovers, dust ruffles and drapery. Some other miscellaneous items that can bring in good profits are tote bags, men's ties, doll clothing, costumes, scarves, bridal veils, sachets and stuffed animals. The possibilities are only limited by your imagination.

Training

If you don't know how to sew or want to update your skills, you can take sewing classes at most community colleges. Your local fabric shop probably has sewing classes as well and there are many books available on the subject.

For more information contact

The Fabricon Company
2021 West Montrose Avenue
Chicago, IL 60618
Home-study course in invisible reweaving methods

Lifetime Career Schools
Dressmaking
101 Harrison Street
Archbald, PA 18403
1-800-423-0239
Offer a home-study correspondence course in dressmaking

Recommended Reading
Fabric Sewing Guide, Claire Shaeffer, Chilton Books, 1994

Hold It!: How to Sew Bags, Totes, Duffels, Pouches and More, Nancy Restuccia, Chilton Books, 1994

Sew News, PJS Publications, Inc., News Plaza, P.O. Box 1790, Peoria, IL 61656, (309) 682-6626—Monthly magazine covering fashion sewing

· EDITOR ·

Career Description
    An editor is a professional who edits material for publishers, such as books, magazines and other written forms of media. Ed-

itors correct spelling, typographical errors and sometimes rewrite text and suggest changes in material written by others.

Career Opportunities

There are many opportunities for freelance editors. Editors are hired by magazines, newspapers, printers, publishers, literary agents, corporations, authors and screenplay writers. Editors may be hired on a per-project basis to proofread text, check grammar and suggest stylistic changes.

Training

Editors must have impeccable reading and writing skills and must be detail oriented. There is no formal training required to become an editor, although more experienced editors tend to get more work.

Recommended Reading

Editors on Editing, Gerald Gross, Grove Press, 1993

The Elements of Editing, Arthur Plotnik, Macmillan, 1982

· ELECTROLOGIST ·

Career Description

An electrologist is a person who permanently removes unwanted hair using special equipment that destroys the hair follicle with a tiny electrical current.

Career Opportunities

Electrology is a relatively new procedure for removing unwanted body hair permanently and safely. Electrologists use a shortwave machine with a very fine needle or wire which puts out a small electrical current and is inserted into the hair follicle.

The small electrical current kills the hair and it is then pulled out with tweezers. The needle does not puncture the skin and is practically painless for the client.

Electrolysis takes the place of temporary hair removal techniques such as waxing, shaving and tweezing, and is rapidly growing in popularity. The hairs are removed one at a time, and it may take several hours for an electrologist to complete one section of the client's body.

Clients come to electrologists to have hair removed from their eyebrows, upper lips, faces, legs, underarms, nostrils, bikini area and anywhere else unwanted hair grows.

Electrologists work under bright lights and often use magnifying lamps because they must work on one hair at a time.

Electrologists usually open their own salons or rent stations in beauty parlors or spas. Trained electrologists are in demand across the country and can make very good money providing this service for clients.

Training

Electrologists must complete a training program (length of programs vary) to learn electrology techniques and how to use the equipment. Some states require electrologists to become licensed, while others do not. Contact your State Board of Cosmetology to find out the requirements in your state. Electrology is taught at some cosmetology schools and by some manufacturers of electrology equipment.

For more information contact

American Electrology Association
106 Oak Ridge Road
Trumbull, CT 06611
Send a SASE for career information and a list of training schools

International Guild of Professional Electrologists
803 N. Main St. Suite A
High Point, NC 27262
(336) 841-6631
Membership organization for professional electrologists

· FACIALIST ·

Career Description

A facial specialist or facialist is a professional skin care expert.

Career Opportunities

Facialists usually own their own salons or work freelance for salons and spas. They perform a wide variety of treatments to the face, such as masks, pore cleansing, acne treatments, facial massages, moisture treatments and chemical peels.

Facilists are skin treatment professionals and know how to help clients with skin problems.

Wrinkle treatments—Many clients depend upon facialists to keep their skin looking young. Some facialists give their clients chemical skin peels, in which a special glycolic acid preparation or alpha-hydroxy treatment is applied to the facial skin. This type of treatment removes dry, damaged outer layers of skin to reveal fresh, new skin. Other wrinkle treatments include oil, herbal and vitamin treatments.

Deep cleansing—Facialists apply deep cleansing mud packs and peel-off masks to clients to remove dirt, grease, oil and other impure properties that clog the skin's pores. Client's with acne problems may see their facialist on a regular basis for cleansing.

Facial massage—Facial massage is a method used to release muscle tension and to help rejuvenate the skin. Facial massage can act as a nonsurgical face-lift and help reduce the appearance of wrinkles and fine lines. Skin tone and appearance can be dramatically improved as well.

Consulting—Facialists consult clients about which skin care products and regimes are best suited for their skin. Some facialists are distributors for a particular skin care line and others develop their own products and treatments.

Training

Facialists must be licensed cosmetologists. Check with your State Board of Cosmetology to find out about the requirements in your state. Most cosmetology schools offer facial training in their curriculums.

For more information contact

The Belavi Institute for Facial Massage
1510 N. Pacific Coast Highway
Laguna Beach, CA 92751
1-800-235-2844
Home-study program to learn facial massage

National Association of Accredited Cosmetology Schools
5201 Leesburg Pike, Suite 205
Falls Church, VA 22041
List of accredited cosmetology schools

· FISHING TACKLE MAKER ·

Career Description

A fishing tackle maker is a craftsman who designs and makes fishing gear such as fishing poles and lures.

Career Opportunities

Making and repairing fishing tackle for a living can be a dream-come-true career for people who enjoy fishing and the outdoors.

Tackle makers create and design fishing rods, lures, bait, hooks and many other pieces of fishing gear. Most tackle makers work out of a small shop or from a home workshop.

Fishing rods—Man's first fishing rods were made from sticks with a piece of bone or live bait on the end to attract fish. Fishing rods have come a long way since primitive times and are now made of aluminum, fiberglass and graphite. Rods can be made to handle different types of fish with their flexibility and strength. There are suppliers of basic "blank" rods that craftsmen use to make their own custom-designed rods from.

Rod repair—Fishing rods can break, splinter, rust and wear out due to use and weather exposure. Rods are expensive to replace and many fishermen take their rods to be repaired and have maintenance checks. Rod repair can be learned from books on the subject.

Lures—Lures are fake bait with hooks attached to them, which attract fish. There are many types of lures on the market and all can be made by a fishing tackle maker. Jigs and bucktails are solid, artificial lures made of lead that have a hook concealed within the body and a skirt or tail of hair or rubber. Spinners and buzzbaits are lures that spin around in the water to attract fish. Soft lures are artificial worms and other "critters" made of plastic and rubber. Wooden lures are hand carved and painted to look like small fish, and have hooks attached to their bodies.

Handcrafted tackle can be sold to bait and tackle shops, which can be found in almost every city in the country. Sport fisherman also frequently buy well-made custom lures. Handcrafted tackle can be sold by mail order to mailing lists of sport fishermen.

A man in Wyoming makes his own custom fishing tackle and has created a novelty item called "the big fly" which he sells out of faster then he can produce. The big fly is a ridiculously large fishing fly which fishermen buy as a joke for friends.

Tackle should be individually wrapped in cellophane bags or in small boxes with your name and address so that you may receive reorders.

Training

There is no training necessary to start making fishing tackle, although better quality tackle made by an experienced craftsman will probably sell better than that made by an amateur. Practice with and testing your lures and tackle will help you develop your skills.

For more information contact

Bass Pro Shops
1935 South Campbell
Springfield, MO 65898
1-800-227-7776
Fly-tying supplies, lure-making supplies and rod-building components

The Netcraft Company
3350 Briarfield Blvd.
Maumee, OH 43537
(419) 472-9826
Hooks, lure-making equipment and supplies, rod components

Recommended Reading
Fiberglass Rod Making, Dale P. Clemens, Winchester Press, 1974

How to Make and Repair Your Own Fishing Tackle, Jim Mayes, Dodd, Mead & Company, Inc., 1986

· FLORAL DESIGNER ·

Career Description

A floral designer is an expert in the art of arranging flowers. A floral designer knows how to aesthetically design arrangements, has a good eye for color and texture and knows where to get flowers.

Career Opportunities

Most floral designers operate their own businesses and work out of a shop or take on freelance assignments. Other floral designers work freelance out of a flower shop.

Floral arrangements—A floral designer can work freelance or for a flower shop, arranging flowers in pretty containers. Holiday arrangements for Christmas, Thanksgiving, Valentine's Day, Mother's Day and birthdays are among the most popular.

Special arrangements—Floral designers often make special flower arrangements, which may include bridal bouquets, corsages, funeral wreaths, nosegays and special table arrangements for parties and banquets.

Weddings—Floral designers are often hired to provide all of the flowers for weddings, such as the bride's bouquet, corsages, table arrangements and floral decorations.

Training

There is no license required to become a floral designer. Some people have a natural talent for putting together beautiful arrangements, but most take classes in floral arrangement which are available through community colleges or can be learned by reading books on the subject. Take a class through community

college, work for a florist or do arrangements for weddings, fu-
nerals, parties, and so on. (you buy the flowers and put together
garlands, nosegays, corsets for proms, etc.).

· FURNITURE RESTORER ·

Career Description
A furniture restorer is a person who repairs and restores old
furniture to its original condition.

Career Opportunities
Furniture restorers specialize in removing old finishes and
paint, revarnishing or repainting, reupholstering and repairing
broken antique furniture.

Most antique furniture pieces are made of woods such as
cherry, mahogany, walnut and maple. Over time, the wood fibers
dry out and layers of paint, varnish and furniture polish can make
the piece look dull and worn.

Furniture restorers always begin by cleaning the furniture to
remove dirt and grease buildup. Restorers then may remove old
paint and varnish. If the wood appears to be dried out, the restorer can apply a coat of linseed oil to renew its surface. The
restorer may then revarnish or repaint the piece.

Many freelance furniture restorers work out of their home
workshops. They pick up furniture from their clients and deliver
it restored when the job is complete. Restorers also buy antique
furniture at auctions and garage sales, restore it and resell it for
a profit. More experienced restorers are able to repair broken
furniture.

Training
There is no formal training or licensing required to become a
furniture restorer. The trade is usually learned by practice and by

reading books about restoration. Beginners should start off restoring small, invaluable pieces to perfect their techniques.

For more information contact

Van Dyke's Restoration
P.O. Box 278
Woonsocket, SD 57385
1-800-843-3320
Complete furniture restoration supplies and books and videos—request catalog

The Woodworkers' Store
4365 Willow Drive
Medina, MN 55340-9701
1-800-279-4441
Mail-order woodworking supplies

Recommended Reading
Care and Repair of Antiques, Thomas H. Ormsbee, Gramercy Publishing

The Complete Book of Furniture Restoration, Tristan Salazar, Crescent Books, 1994

Popular Woodworking, 1320 Galaxy Way, Concord, CA 84520—Magazine for woodworkers

· GAMING SERVICE TECHNICIAN ·

Career Description
A gaming service technician is a trained professional who repairs, services and maintains gambling machines.

Career Opportunities

Qualified and professional gaming technicians are in demand around the world. There are thousands of casinos in the United States alone, and each of those casinos houses thousands of gambling machines, such as video poker, slot machines, video blackjack and keno. These machines break down or malfunction and require regular servicing by trained professionals. As a repair technician you can find work in states that allow gambling, at some Indian reservations where casinos are legal, on some cruise ships and in other countries.

Most technicians work for casinos on a freelance basis and respond to service and maintenance calls. Some large casinos hire technicians on a full-time basis if they have a lot of gambling machines in their establishment.

Training

You must complete a training program and become a certified gaming repair technician before you can start working. All of the training programs require you to attend a school to receive hands-on training. Technicians learn basic and advanced electronics, gaming machine technology and about computers.

For more information contact

Morrison College
140 Washington Street
Reno, NV 89503
(702) 323-4145
Career training for gaming equipment technicians

· GENEALOGIST ·

Career Description

A genealogist is a person who traces the family ancestries and histories of clients. The word "genealogy" comes from the Greek word *genealogia*, which means "pedigree" or "race." This career is good for people who enjoy research.

Career Opportunities

Tracing the history of a family can be confusing and time-consuming. Many people want to know about their ancestors, but shy away from the long and sometimes difficult process of researching and digging up facts. Professional genealogists are hired by people to research and write genealogical reports and trace family trees to preserve the history of the family.

Training

There is no training or licensing required to become a genealogist. There are many books and computer software programs available to help genealogists in their research. As with any career, the more experience and practice you have, the easier the work will be.

For more information contact

The Everton Publishers
P.O. Box 368
Logan, UT 84321
Genealogy books and periodicals

The Genealogical Society
35 North West Temple
Salt Lake City, UT 84150
Information about genealogy

National Genealogical Society
4527 17th Street North
Arlington, VA 22207-2399

(703) 525-0050
Research center and library for members

Recommended Reading
Guide to Genealogy Software, Donna Przecha and Joan Lo-
wrey, Genealogical Publishing, 1993

International Vital Records Handbook, Thomas J. Kemp, Genealogical Publishing, 1990

Searching for Your Ancestors, Gilbert Harry Doane and
James B. Bell, University of Minnesota Press, 1992

· HAIRSTYLIST ·

Career Description
A hairstylist is a trained professional who cuts and styles the
hair of clients. A hairstylist may also permanent wave, tint, color
and lighten a client's hair.

Career Opportunities
Stylists are trained to work with hair. Stylists must attend
school and learn proper cutting techniques. Stylists are professionals who know how to give clients the right cut for their face
shape. Stylists are able to work with fine, straight, coarse, curly,
wavy and frizzy hair, making their clients look their best. Some
clients have professional hairstylists color, tint, lighten and permanent wave their hair. These processes are done by professional
stylists who have been trained to apply such preparations.

Stylists usually rent workstations in beauty salons, but some
stylists own their own shops. Stylists can also find work in hotels,
on cruise ships and in spas. Clients will often hire their stylists to

set, curl and style their hair for special occasions. Stylists may also find work styling hair for the television and movie industry.

Training

To become a hairstylist, you must become a licensed cosmetologist. Contact the State Board of Cosmetology in your state to find out the licensing requirements. Training programs vary in length in each state. Many cosmetology schools offer evening programs. To find a school in your area, look in the yellow pages under the headings "Schools" or "Beauty." You can also write to the National Association of Accredited Cosmetology Schools for a list of schools nationwide.

For more information contact

National Association of Accredited Cosmetology Schools
5201 Leesburg Pike, Suite 205
Falls Church, VA 22041
List of accredited cosmetology schools

Reccomended Reading

The Complete Book of Braids, Linda Sheilds Ksiazek, Longmeadow Press, 1991

Robert Renn's Complete Book of Hair Coloring, Robert Renn, Random House, 1979

· HEADHUNTER ·

Career Description

A headhunter is a person who finds qualified individuals seeking work and matches them up with employers seeking such individuals.

Career Opportunities

Many businesses often need to fill a position right away or don't want to spend the time and money to advertise for employees. Other employers may need people with special skills or training. Whatever the situation, the headhunting business is booming.

One headhunter in Los Angeles places ads in local papers and magazines offering jobs and placement. He runs another ad in the same papers geared to attract businesses offering qualified employees, domestic help, laborers and executives. He receives calls from people seeking work and keeps their résumés on file. At the same time, employers call him to fill their various positions. He matches up qualified employees with companies. He signs an agreement with the employer that states that if they hire an employee that he sent to them for an interview, the employer will pay him the equivalent of one week's salary for the employee. He then offers a ninety-day guarantee on the employee and offers a free replacement if the employee does not stay or it doesn't work out.

Training

There is no training necessary to become a headhunter. Headhunters should be familiar with the job market and should establish and maintain communication with personnel managers of local businesses.

· HEALTH PRODUCTS DISTRIBUTOR ·

Career Description

A health product distributor is a person who works freelance as a salesperson for a manufacturer of products.

Career Opportunities

The salesperson usually finds a product he or she believes in and signs up to become a representative. As a representative, he or she can buy the company's products at wholesale prices and resell them at retail prices to individuals.

Some health products companies have multilevel marketing or "pyramid" programs where the representative signs up and then gets others to sell products. The representative receives a percentage of proceeds from the representatives beneath him or her.

Representatives may sell a wide range of health and beauty products, such as vitamins, minerals, exercise equipment, water filters, creams, soaps, cosmetics, cleaning products, diet foods and many more.

To get started, find a product that you've tried and like. Contact the manufacturer of the product and find out what kind of programs they offer for distributors. Many large companies offer free training to their freelance representatives. You don't have to limit yourself to selling only one product for one company. Distributors often sell entire lines of products or several products from different manufacturers.

Training

There is no experience necessary to become a health products distributor. Sales skills are helpful and there are many books available on the subject.

· HEIR FINDER ·

Career Description

An heir finder is a person who finds situations where the money of a deceased person is being held by government and private organizations and gets it to its rightful heir.

Career Opportunities

Each state has a department of abandoned and unclaimed property files. When a person dies and has not left a will and the state can't contact a relative, the person's property and money are given to the state to be held. Banks, estates, pension funds and other sources of money are given to the state to be held until a rightful heir claims the money.

Sometimes people don't know that their deceased relative exists, and heir finders trace the deceased's closest heir. The heir finder traces the nearest relative through genealogy or address books and contacts the correct person. The correct heir must then be verified and established.

Before the heir finder reveals who the heir is, he or she works out an agreement with the person to disclose the information only after they have written up a contract for the heir finder to receive a percentage of the money as his or her pay.

Training

Some states require that heir finders have a private investigator's license before they will release their lists of abandoned and unclaimed property. There is no training necessary to become an heir finder, although knowing investigating techniques would be helpful. See the listing in this book for Private Investigator.

For more information contact your State Department of Abandoned and Unclaimed Property to get the laws and regulations in your area.

· HOME INSPECTOR ·

Career Description

A home inspector is a person who inspects homes for purchasers, lenders and realtors who are buying or selling homes or property.

Career Opportunities

Consumers are cautious these days when buying a home and often hire home inspectors to ensure that the home or property passes a general inspection before they buy.

A good home inspector relies on common sense, ethics and some learned technical know-how.

One out of ten home buyers spends more than one thousand dollars in the first year of owning a home on repairs that should have been handled by the previous owner. Hiring a home inspector to give an honest opinion of the home's condition can save the new home owner much hassle and thousands of dollars down the road.

There is currently a shortage of qualified home inspectors to meet consumer demand. There are only a few thousand home inspectors working today in the United States and most property buyers are now having home inspections before they buy.

Home inspectors are hired by real estate agents, real estate appraisers, banks, relocation companies and, most commonly, by buyers and sellers of residential and commercial property. An inspector checks many areas of the property for problems. Some of the areas an inspector looks at are roofs, skylights, chimneys, rain gutters, erosion, drainage structures, walls, windows, doors, landscaping, trees, garages, garage door openers, paved areas, termite and insect infestation, attics, basements, crawl spaces, electrical systems, plumbing systems, water pressure, heating and A/C systems, water heaters, ventilation, evaporative coolers, caulking, weather stripping, sprinklers, foundations and air ducts—to name a few. It is a good idea to involve clients in the inspection by having them walk through the home as the inspection is being conducted so they can see what is being done. The inspector checks these and other areas of the property and submits a written report that specifies any problems that were found. The report must be as accurate as possible. This written report is then given to the person who hired the inspector. Home inspectors should never give verbal reports to their clients.

Training

Some states require home inspectors to be licensed. Check with your state regulatory agency to find out about requirements in your area. Whether or not your state requires you to be licensed, you must be trained to become a home inspector in order to provide your clients with the best possible inspection and to avoid lawsuits.

For more information contact

The School of Home Inspection
430 Technology Parkway
Norcross, GA 30092
1-800-223-4542
Correspondence course on home inspecting

Builder's Book, Inc.
8001 Canoga Avenue
Canoga Park, CA 91304
1-800-273-7375
Books, forms and courses about home inspection—ask for catalog

· HOMEOPATH/NATUROPATH ·

Career Description

Homeopaths and naturopaths are practitioners of natural and holistic healing.

Career Opportunities

More and more people are becoming aware that chemical, radiation and surgical treatments of disease by medical doctors do not always translate into better health for the consumer. This awareness combined with the high costs of modern medicine has lead to the search for safe and natural healing practices, thus creating a huge demand for trained holistic healers.

Homeopathic and naturopathic counselors and consultants are educated practitioners of alternative healing.

Naturopathic counselor, consultant or doctor—Naturopaths help patients to overcome health problems through holistic nutrition using whole foods, herbal, vitamin and mineral therapies. They may help patients with alternative treatments for cancer, arthritis and many other ailments. Counselors usually have their own private practices and consult with doctors, chiropractors and dentists to help patients overcome health problems.

Homeopathic counselor, consultant or doctor—Homeopaths help patients overcome health problems using natural home remedies. Most homeopaths have their own private practices.

Naturopathy veterinarian—A professional who uses natural and holistic healing processes on animals.

Training

Training is required to be a professional homeopathic or naturopathic counselor, consultant or doctor. You can earn a bachelor's, master's or doctoral degree in either field.

For more information contact

The Clayton College of Natural Health
2140 11th Avenue South, # 305
Birmingham, AL 35205
1-800-995-4590
Homeopathic and naturopathic correspondence courses and college degree programs

Recommended Reading

The Complete Guide to Homeopathy, Dr. Christopher Hammond, Penguin Books, 1995

Encyclopedia of Natural Medicine, Michael Murray, N.D. and Joseph Pizzorno, N.D., Prima Publishing, 1995

New Choices in Natural Healing, Rodale Press, Inc., 1995

· HOUSEHOLD MANAGER ·

Career Description

Household management is a new and unique career that entails the supervision and operation of large, spacious homes and estates. Many of the families that hire household and estate managers are incredibly busy individuals who need management support to oversee the everyday demands of running a home. Today's employers in this field are looking for individuals who love to travel and are educated, professional, career oriented and interested in making a difference.

Career Opportunities

Household staff usually work for families or individuals on a permanent basis, although short-term and temporary assignments are sometimes available. In today's marketplace, there are many household management positions available. Unfortunately there are not enough trained professionals to fill those positions. Experienced and trained household management staff can find employment with a competitive salary and sometimes benefit packages.

Estate manager—An estate manager holds an administrative position in a large household (usually over 20,000 square feet) which oversees the activity of all other household employees, such as maids, cooks, and so on. The estate manager must know how to perform all household duties and may hire, train and supervise other employees. The manager keeps things running smoothly in the household.

Household manager—A household manager is responsible for the overall operation and maintenance of a home and performs the duties of the butler and housekeeper. Household managers must be trained in cleaning; cooking; etiquette; entertaining; clothing care; security; management and training of other household employees; and care of automobiles, antiques, silver and other valuables; and all other maintenance aspects of the home.

Butler or personal assistant—Butlers usually work for the man of the house and perform the duties of a valet, including cooking, light cleaning, greeting visitors, clothing care and help with personal errands. The woman's counterpart is called a personal assistant and performs similar duties. The butler or personal assistant may travel with his or her employer and is the employer's right-hand man (or woman).

Household Chef—The household chef is a trained culinary professional who provides meals for the family. Household chefs are usually knowledgeable in household entertaining, setting formal tables, flower arrangements, wines and other household etiquette.

Training

Household staff should have experience and training in home economics.

For more information contact

Starkey International Institute for Household Management
1350 Logan Street
Denver, CO 80203
1-800-888-4904

Training programs and certification of household managers and career information

Reccomended Reading

Mary Ellen's Clean House, Mary Ellen Pinkham, Crown Books, 1993

· INDEX WRITER ·

Career Description

An index writer is a person who cross-references key words in the back of a book to the pages where those topics are mentioned.

Career Opportunities

Indexing is systematically arranging entries in the back of a book to enable the reader to locate information in the book. Indexes list key words to help readers find information quickly by referring them to a particular section, paragraph or sentence in the book.

Indexers are trying to provide answers to unasked questions that may come from the reader of the book. The indexer must therefore try to place him or herself in the shoes of the reader and make the index as informative and thorough as possible.

Index writers are hired by publishers and writers to write indexes for books. Before a book is printed, indexers receive a set of page proofs, which are images of the actual pages of the book as they will appear, including the final page numbers. The indexer reads the proofs and makes lists of headings and subheadings that will appear in the index of the book, including all pertinent references. After completing the rough index, the indexer edits it for structure, clarity and consistency and then formats and proofreads it. The completed index is then returned to the client in hard-copy form or on disk.

Indexers must be able to work quickly since this is usually the last step in the process of producing a book, before it is printed. Tight deadlines are common for indexers.

Training

There is no formal training required to become an indexer, although indexers should complete a training program to learn the proper techniques of indexing.

For more information contact

The American Society of Indexers
P.O. Box 48267, Department A
Seattle, WA 98148-0267
(206) 241-9196
Information about indexing careers and schools and newsletter for indexers, *Key Words*

Susan Holbert Indexing Services
24 Harris Street
Waltham, MA 02452-6105
(718) 893-0514
Complete home-study training program for indexers, including video workshop, course book, sample forms, marketing program and telephone consultation

· INTERIOR DECORATOR ·

Career Description

An interior decorator is a professional who enhances the aesthetic appearance of interiors of homes and buildings through decorating and coordination. An interior decorator may be hired to purchase new furniture, drapery, and artwork and to help the client choose coordinating colors of paint, wallpaper and flooring and to make a wide variety of other interior decisions.

Career Opportunities

This career offers excellent opportunities for the freelance professional. Most professional decorators work from their own private studio and visit clients interested in redecorating.

Decorators will work in private homes, businesses, restaurants and retail stores, helping their clients to achieve their decorating goals within a specified budget.

A good example of a decorator's work would be consulting a home owner who wants to change her home from a contemporary to a country theme. The decorator would assist the client in choosing new furniture and coordinating colors in the home to suit the client's taste. Another possible client would be a new restaurant owner. The building was a diner and the new owner is opening a Mexican restaurant. The decorator would locate Mexican furniture and might coordinate the painting of the interior to look like adobe.

A good decorator is a good listener. He or she knows where to purchase all types of furniture and accessories. He or she also knows about painting, wallpaper, flooring, upholstery and who to call to do such work. The decorator can get the job done, on time and on budget, and always has satisfied customers.

The decorator keeps up with current trends and knows the classics cold. He or she can create an aesthetically pleasing space. The decorator comes to the client armed with fabric swatches, paint samples and photos of different furniture styles.

Training

There is no formal education or licensing required to become an interior decorator. You can take college courses on decorating if you wish, but this is not mandatory. If you are not familiar with the field, you can begin your career by working as an apprentice for a decorator or interior designer. You should also read books about decorating and learn about trends, antiques, painting, flooring, upholstery, and so on. Subscribe to decorating magazines and keep up with new trends—these publications will also help you develop new theme ideas and attractive room plans. You can take classes in decorating at city and community colleges. Most interior decorators carry books that are full of photos of their previous work. Your reputation and a portfolio full of happy clients will get you far.

· INSURANCE FRAUD INVESTIGATOR ·

Career Description

Insurance fraud investigators are hired freelance by insurance companies, attorneys and private individuals to investigate claims when questions arise as to their legitimacy.

Career Opportunities

When an individual files a claim, the insurance company or party being sued must pay a settlement, and if they believe the claim to be fraudulent, they will hire outside investigators to look into the matter in order to save money and prosecute false claims.

Personal injury—Many phony insurance claims are worker's compensation claims or personal injury claims. An example is the man who claims he was hurt on the job and therefore cannot work and is suing for benefits and damages.

When an investigator is hired, he or she is given the name of the individual to be investigated. The investigator will then track down the individual who filed the claim and survey his activity. Say a man filed a worker's compensation claim after "hurting his leg" on the job. The man is tracked down and followed by an investigator and found kick-starting his motorcycle when he should have been in bed recovering. The investigator catches this act on videotape and with a still camera and the assignment is complete. The evidence is presented in court, and needless to say, the claimant does not receive his settlement and is prosecuted for filing a false claim.

General insurance fraud—Another type of insurance fraud that investigators may be hired to look into includes claims of non-existent property, staged burglaries, duplicate coverage and fine art fraud. Rising insurance costs have made it more important than ever to make sure that a claim is legitimate, especially given the skill and creativity of those inclined toward fraudulent activity. Often an insurance fraud investigator is the only way to uncover such illegal activity.

Training

In some states it may be necessary to have a private investigator's license, depending upon the type of insurance fraud work you are doing. Contact your state regulatory agency to find out what is required in your area.

For more information contact

The Association of Certified Fraud Examiners
716 West Avenue
Austin, TX 78701
1-800-245-3321
Fraud training seminars and information

Claim School, Inc.
6319 West Slauson Avenue
Culver City, CA 90230

(310) 390-1029
Books for insurance fraud investigators

Merlin Information Services
215 S. Complex Drive
Kalispell, MT 59901
1-800-367-6646
Public record databases on CD-ROM

National Association of Legal Investigators
P.O. Box 905
Grand Blanc, MI 48439
1-800-266-6254
Information and certification program for legal investigators

William C. Dear Agency
2720 Stemmons Fwy, Suite 711
Dallas, TX 75207
(214) 630-9834
Seminars, videos and books about fraud investigation

· INTERPRETER ·

Career Description

Interpreters are people who are able to fluently translate written and spoken words from one language into another.

Career Opportunities

There are many opportunities for interpreters in today's global marketplace. Effective and clear communication is vital in business and legal matters, in the medical field and in many other areas of our lives. A person who can translate communications from one language into another is valuable, and many people are making a living using their multilingual skills.

Being able to translate other languages is a bonus in any career, whether or not you choose to make it your sole profession.

Business translation—Many businesses who deal with foreign countries hire freelance interpreters to present, negotiate and close business deals. Written material such as proposals and contracts may also be translated for smooth and clear business deals.
Publishing—Publishers frequently hire translators to translate written material in English, such as books and magazines, into foreign languages and vice versa.
Legal interpretation—County, state and federal agencies frequently hire translators to interpret in our bilingual world. These agencies include justice courts, immigration and naturalization departments, medical facilities, insurance companies, financial institutions, law enforcement agencies, customs and other agencies that are legally bound to interpret communications.

Training

To become an interpreter you must speak and write fluently in two or more languages. If you want to learn another language, there are many classes and programs available through community colleges, books and tapes.

· INVESTMENT CLUB ORGANIZER ·

Career Description

An investment club organizer is a person who starts and operates a group of people who jointly invest in the stock market as a group. Most investment clubs invest in the stock market because it offers better returns than other types of investments. In an investment group, the members each put in a small amount of money toward the total group investment and share the responsibility of researching investments. Groups meet once a week or once a month. This is a good part-time career and a great introduction to the stock market for beginners.

Career Opportunities

In these tough times we all could use a little extra cash. Starting an investment club is a great way to get into the stock market with a minimal investment. The organizer of the group usually contacts his or her friends, family, neighbors and associates to ask them to join the club. The group members agree to donate a specified amount of investment money each month to buy stocks. Four main positions are assigned to club members: president, vice president, treasurer and secretary. The leader of the group assigns the members research projects and other duties such as studying different industries and pulling company profiles. The group members decide which industries they would like to invest in. Examples of some of the industries that a group might research are oil, utilities and technology. After the industries are decided upon, assigned members can pull company profiles within that industry. Companies will provide annual and quarterly reports free of charge. Group members then go over the findings of their research and make investment decisions by voting.

Kate Gordon started an investment club in her neighborhood as a part-time career. She recommends a maximum of sixteen members per club. One stock that her club bought doubled in value within four months. Kate says that investment clubs are a great way to learn about the stock market and make some extra money. She has learned valuable money management skills through her efforts with the club, which have helped her to make some smart investments with her own personal savings. She added that investment clubs are also a fun, social activity. Her club has hosted teas and holiday dinners for members.

The amount of money that each member invests is a decision

agreed upon by the club members. Some clubs ask that their members invest as little as twenty-five dollars a month and other groups ask for more from their members. The organizer of the club opens a bank account in the club's name and buys the stocks that the club members agree upon. Stocks can be bought through discount brokers who will sell stocks at a lower than usual rate. Discount brokers can be found in the yellow pages under "Stock Brokers."

Training

There is no training or licensing required to start and operate an investment club. There are many books available on the subject. You can also read money magazines and stock reports in the newspaper. The Internet can also be a valuable research tool. Many experts are willing to share information with beginners.

For more information contact

The National Association of Investment Clubs (NAIC)
711 West Thirteen Mile Road
Madison Heights, MN 48071
(248) 583-6242
Investment education for individuals and investment clubs

Recommended Reading

The Beardstown Ladies' Common Sense Investment Guide, Hyperion, 1995

Starting and Running a Profitable Investment Club, Thomas E. O'Hara and Kenneth S. Janke, Sr., Times Books, 1996

· JEWELRY DESIGNER ·

Career Description

A jewelry designer is a skilled professional who designs, makes and repairs jewelry. Some jewelry designers use precious metals and stones or cut gems, while others design paste or costume jewelry.

Career Opportunities

Jewelry throughout history has been used by man as a symbol of status, success, honor, love and beauty. Today jewelry is worn to express love, culture and beauty. Jewelry is sold in every city in every state, and business will continue to boom.

Designer—A designer is a person who sketches ideas for jewelry, either precious or costume. This jewelry is either custom-made for a client or mass-produced for the general public.

Craftsman—A craftsman is a person who creates the finished product from the designer's sketches or models.

Gem cutter and setter—Setters and cutters of gems are jewelers who specialize in cutting, shaping and mounting precious and semiprecious stones.

Repairer—A repairer is a person who specializes in repairing jewelry items.

Appraiser—An appraiser is a person who is able to determine what an item of jewelry is worth.

Training

Training to become a jewelry designer is available through schools, or you can begin your career by working as an apprentice for an established jeweler. Costume jewelry requires no formal training and you can learn by reading books on the subject of jewelry making, which are available in bookstores and libraries.

For more information contact

The Bookshelf
P.O. Box 6925
Ventura, CA 93006
Write for catalog of jewelry making and repair books

Eloxite Corporation
806 Tenth Street
Wheatland, WY 82201
(307) 322-3050
Jewelry making supplies and tools by mail order

Gemological Institute of America
1660 Stewart Street
P.O. Box 2110
Santa Monica, CA 90407-2110
1-800-421-7250
Correspondence classes in jewelry design, gemology and repair

Jewelers of America
1271 Avenue of the Americas
Rockefeller Center
New York, NY 10020
Information about careers in jewelry

TSI
101 Nickerson Street
Seattle, WA 98109
1-800-426-9984
Suppliers of beads, findings, gems, waxes and tools for jewelry making, ask for catalog

Recommended Reading

The Design and Creation of Jewelry, Robert Von Neumann, Chilton, 1982

Fashion Accessories, S.C.M. Publications, Inc., 65 West Main Street, Bergenfield, NJ 07621-1696, (201) 384-3336—Monthly newspaper covering costume and fashion jewelry

Jewelry Crafts, Miller Magazines Inc., 4880 Market Street, Ventura, CA 93003—Monthly magazine about jewelry making

Jewelry Design Sourcebook, Diana Scarsbrick, Van Nostrand Reinhold, 1989

Jewelry Making, Gill Clement, Chartwell Books, Inc., 1994

· LAMP MAKER AND REPAIRER ·

Career Description

A lamp maker is a person who designs, builds and creates lamps. A lamp repairer is a person who fixes lamps and lighting. The two careers can be easily combined.

Career Opportunities

Lamp makers create and design table lamps, floor lamps and hanging lamps of all shapes, sizes and designs.

Bases—Lamp bases can be made out of wood, ceramics, decorative brass, marble and stained glass. Nearly any hollow object, such as a favorite vase or figurine, can be used as a base, as long as wiring can be run through it. Ready-made bases can be bought from suppliers, ranging from porcelain to metal antique replicas. One lamp maker in Los Angeles has been using antique teapots as lamp bases and adding beautiful lamp shades for his limited-edition lamp collection. His one-of-a-kind lamps sell faster than he can create them, in gift shops and craft fairs.

Shades—Lamp makers also design and create lamp shades using a wide variety of fabrics. Silk, lace, cotton, vinyl and even leather are popular fabrics. Lamp shades can be custom-made to match furniture patterns using the same fabric or matching colors and textures. Lamp shade forms are very similar and easy to make with a little practice. Lamp makers usually buy shade frames and cover them with fabric. Some lamp makers hand-paint designs on their shades.

A woman in Northern California creates replicas of Victorian-era lamp shades with silk and beaded fringe. She displays her breathtaking shades on old-fashioned brass bases and makes several hundred dollars' profit on each of her handcrafted lamps. She admits that the beading takes a long time, but she thoroughly enjoys her work.

Another shade maker designs and sells a line of contemporary lamps. His sleek shades sit upon black wooden bases and are covered in solid blacks or leopard prints. His exclusive line of lamps began as a humble, home-based business and he now supplies a major furniture store and has moved his operation into a large studio.

Other Opportunities—Stained glass Tiffany-style lamps are increasing in popularity. To find out more about the art of stained glass, see the entry in this book for Stained Glass Artist.
Repair—Lamp makers may also consider repairing broken lamps. Lamp makers already understand the simple wiring of lamps and are able to repair most lamp problems with ease. One lamp repairer specializes in rewiring antique lamps and updating their electrical systems. He sells his lamps at antiques shows for several hundred dollars each. His business keeps him busy year-round.

Recommended Reading
   Basic Wiring, Sunset Books, 1995

   Lamp Shades, K. Cargill, Random House, 1996

Step-by-Step Basic Wiring, Better Homes and Gardens Books, 1980

· LAWNMOWER REPAIR TECHNICIAN ·

Career Description

A lawnmower repair technician is a person who repairs broken or poorly running lawnmowers and other outdoor power equipment, such as chain saws, small tractors and weed wackers.

Career Opportunities

Lawnmower repairers usually work out of their own shops or home workshops and do repairs on power equipment such as replacing motors, sharpening blades and performing maintenance tune-ups. The broken equipment can either be picked up by the repair person or dropped off at the repair shop. Gardeners, hardware shops and garden supply shops are a good source of business referrals.

Outdoor power equipment is expensive to replace. Some repairers buy and repair old, broken power equipment and resell it for a profit.

Training

There is no license required to become a lawnmower repair person. Repairers should be familiar with outdoor power equipment and how it works. Some repairers start off as apprentices to learn the business. There are many good books and manufacturer's manuals available on the subject of repairing outdoor power equipment.

Recommended Reading

The Complete Book of Lawnmower Repair, Paul Dempsey, TAB Books, 1975

Handbook of Lawn Mower Repair, Franklynn Peterson, Emerson Books, 1984

How to Sharpen Anything, Don Geary, TAB Books, 1983 Sharpening blades and replacing old motors

Sincere's Lawn Mower Service, William Ewers, Sincere Press, 1971

Small Engine Maintenance and Repair for Outdoor Power Equipment, Arthur Darack, Prentice-Hall, Inc., 1984

Walk-behind Lawn Mower, 3rd ed., Intertec Publishing Corporation, 1987

You Fix It: Lawn Mowers, Carmine C. Castellano and Clifford P. Seitz, Arco Publishing, 1978

· LICENSING AGENT ·

Career Description

A licensing agent is a person who represents the firms who hold the titles to patented or copyrighted products or material, and arranges manufacturing of the product or distribution of it to other firms, individuals or companies. Every time a copyrighted or patented product is manufactured and sold, the licensing agent receives a royalty as his or her fee for arranging the deal.

Licensing agents find products that they are familiar with or interested in and contact the manufacturers with a letter stating that would like to work with them to license overseas companies to make their product and arrange that the manufacturer will be paid a suitable royalty. When an agent has an interested company, they then contact overseas firms that handle similar products and advertise that they have a U.S. company seeking to sell overseas rights to make their product. When an agent gets an interested party, they arrange to go ahead with a licensing deal. The usual fee for licensing and manufacturing or building a product is 10 percent of the selling price of the item. The licensing agent should get at least 10 percent of the amount the U.S. firm or other domestic firm receives, or 1 percent of the total amount.

Contact a licensing attorney to help you with the agreement and paperwork.

Career Opportunities

There are basically two types of licensing agents: product and industrial.

Products—A licensing agent who represents products contacts the owner of the copyright, patent or trademark and arranges deals with overseas firms to manufacture and distribute the item.
Industrial—An industrial licensing agent represents machinery and makes deals for the owner of the patent with overseas companies to manufacture the machinery.

Training

There is no license required to become a licensing agent, nor is there any formal training. There is, however, a publication available about the career.

For more information contact

International Wealth Success
P.O. Box 186
Merrick, NY 11566
(516) 766-5850
Publication about becoming a licensing agent

· LIQUIDATOR ·

Career Description

Traditionally, liquidators bought distressed or unwanted merchandise at rock-bottom prices (usually 10 percent of retail value or less) from manufacturers and resold it to retailers or wholesalers for a profit. The term "liquidate" means to settle the affairs of a business that is closing by selling off its assets and stock. Nowadays, many manufacturers "liquidate" their overstocked merchandise to raise money, and most of them are not by any means going out of business. You can become a liquidator right now with no money in your pocket.

Career Opportunities

A liquidator may get started simply by approaching a manufacturer and inquiring if the manufacturer has any overstocked merchandise that he or she wishes to liquidate. If the liquidator is interested in the merchandise, he or she then settles on a fair price with the manufacturer and asks to have the exclusive right to sell the merchandise. The liquidator then marks up the merchandise accordingly and offers the entire inventory to buyers. The liquidator's buyers can be wholesalers, exporters, retail stores and even other liquidators. The liquidator has the buyer pay him for the merchandise, then pays the seller and arranges transportation, and keeps the difference as profit.

A young woman recently became a liquidator and arranged a very profitable deal her first week. She found a manufacturer of outdoor patio umbrellas who had one hundred overstocked umbrellas in his inventory that had a retail value of $150 each. He agreed to sell them to the liquidator for $15 each. The liquidator found a retail shop willing to buy these umbrellas for $68 dollars each. The liquidator collected the money from the buyer and paid the seller, making a profit of $5,300 all for a few hours' work. There is merchandise available in every city in every state.

You just need to call the manufacturers to find it and then find buyers. After a short time, you will have built up your own network of buyers and sellers.

Training

There is no training or licensing required to become a liquidator.

For more information contact

Association of Certified Liquidators
1476 Clara Avenue
Columbus, OH 43211-2624
Write for information about their excellent training program, *How to Liquidate Your Way to a Fortune*

· LITERARY AGENT ·

Career Description

A literary agent is a person who represents writers and their work and sells it to publishers.

Career Opportunities

A good literary agent is able to negotiate the best terms possible for the sale of his or her client's work.

The standard fee a literary agent charges is 15 percent of the writer's earnings upon sale of the work. Any agent who advertises that he or she is seeking authors to represent will almost immediately find him or herself drowning in a sea of unpublished manuscripts. After reading the manuscripts, a literary agent chooses the ones that the agent feels he or she can sell, draws up an author/agent contract and begins to submit the work to publishers. After a short while, the literary agent will develop a feel for what each publisher is looking for and will know what editors to send different types of work to. Some agents specialize in handling certain genres, such as romance, horror, science fiction, contemporary fiction, children's books, educational, health, how-to and business.

Training

There is no license or formal training required to become a literary agent. An excellent way to learn the business and establish connections to publishers is to work as an intern or assistant for an established literary agent.

Recommended Reading

The Aggressive Writer's Guide, Sally Smith & Associates, 662 W. Huntington Drive, Suite 898, Monrovia, CA 91016—A complete guide on book publishing

How to Be Your Own Literary Agent, Richard Curtis, Houghton Mifflin Company, 1984

The Writer's Guide to Book Editors, Publishers, and Literary Agents, Jeff Herman, Prima Publishing, updated yearly

The Writer's Market, Writer's Digest Books, F&W Publications, updated yearly

· LOAN BROKER ·

Career Description

A loan broker is a person who acts as an intermediary between borrowers and lenders. Brokers are paid a fee for arranging all types of loans for borrowers. At some time or another, most people and businesses need to borrow money, and this is where a loan broker comes in.

Career Opportunities

Loan brokers can arrange loans for individuals, small businesses or corporations. After the recent S&L scandal, the federal government imposed tighter restrictions on savings-and-loans and banking institutions. As a result, the average borrower who used to obtain financing from S&L's or banks is now being turned down. Brokers are now receiving 40 percent more loan requests than before and a majority of those requests are for excellent real estate and business projects.

Brokers receive their potential borrower's loan proposals and match them up with lenders such as private investors, life insurance companies, mortgage bankers, private companies, credit companies and many other sources of loans.

Most loan brokers have their own businesses, but some work for brokerage firms. The income potential for this business is very high while the start-up investment is minimal.

Training

There is no licensing required to become a loan broker. This career can be started immediately from your own home, on a full- or part-time basis. There are training programs and books about loan brokering available to help you get started.

For more information contact

American Bankers Association
Customer Service Center
P.O. Box 70064
Baltimore, MD 21279-0064
(202) 663-5087
Write for brochure, Building Your Future—Banking Is the Answer

Wes-State Mortgage
1450 West 7th Avenue
Eugene, OR 97402
1-800-356-0473
Loan broker training programs, books and information about
careers in brokering

· LOCKSMITH ·

Career Description

A locksmith is a person whose work is making and repairing
locks and keys. Trained individuals earn top dollar for their services. Locksmiths are in demand in every city in every state.

Career Opportunities

There are millions of homes, businesses and autos with locks
that need to be repaired and have keys made for them. The number of locks and keys in use grows larger every day. Every time
a key is lost or an employee leaves, locks may be changed and
keys must be replaced. People also need spare keys made.

Most keys are made from soft metals that are not meant to
last. Soft metals are used in order to protect fragile lock mecha-
nisms, but they usually result in frequent breakage. As a professional locksmith you will learn how to take key impressions, cut
keys, make spare keys, repair and install locks and deadbolts and
change safe combinations.

Locksmiths are needed on new construction projects, both
commercial and residential, to install new locks, and are called
upon in the case of home and car lock-outs. Hotels and motels
also frequently require the services of a locksmith. Other unusual
opportunities for locksmiths can be found making keys for and/
or repairing luggage and briefcase locks, vending machine locks
and combination locks.

As a locksmith, you can run your own freelance business or

you may take a job with a large institution such as a hospital or university, many of which keep a full-time locksmith on staff.

Physical limitations are no barrier to the trade. Locksmithing is generally light, easy work. You can work locally on your own schedule, with little travel required. There is no heavy lifting or hard labor involved. A locksmith can easily run this business from a home office or workshop.

The overhead costs of operating as a locksmith are considerably low.

Training

In order to be a professional locksmith, you will need to learn the trade. You may either enroll in a locksmithing course or start as an apprentice with an established locksmith.

For more information contact

Associated Locksmiths of America
3003 Live Oak Street
Dallas, TX 74204

Foley-Belsaw Institute
6301 Equitable Road
Kansas City, MO 64120
1-800-821-3452
Wholesaler of locksmithing supplies, offers a mail correspondence diploma program in locksmithing

The National Locksmith Magazine
1533 Burgundy Parkway
Streamwood, IL 60107
Books, software programs and magazines about locksmithing

National Locksmith Suppliers Association
1900 Arch Street
Philadelphia, PA 19103

· MAIL ORDER SALESPERSON ·

Career Description

A mail order salesperson is someone who sells merchandise or information through the mail.

Career Opportunities

Mail order selling can be a profitable part-time career that requires little effort and attention. Thousands of products are sold through the mail every day and you can get started almost immediately. To be successful in the mail order business, you need to sell a product that people need and want. Get a post office box, place advertisements in the paper, send catalogs to mailing lists and make sure that you'll make a profit (buy cheap enough and remember postage).

Training

There is no training required to become a mail order salesperson. If you are selling goods by mail, you will need to get a seller's permit, which you can apply for at your State Board of Equalization. There are many books about mail order selling available at libraries and bookstores.

Recommended Reading

Building a Mail Order Business: A Complete Manual for Success, William A. Cohen, Wiley, 1985

How Mail Order Fortunes Are Made, 4th ed., Alfred Stern, Arco Publishing, 1984

How to Get Rich in Mail Order, Melvin Powers, Wilshire Book Company, 1980

How to Start and Operate a Mail-Order Business, Julian L. Simon, McGraw-Hill, 1987

Mail Order Success Secrets, Tyler G. Hicks, Prima Publishing, 1994

Selling By Mail: An Entrepreneurial Guide to Direct Marketing, John W. Graham and Susan K. Jones, Macmillan, 1985

· MANICURIST/PEDICURIST ·

Career Description

A manicurist/pedicurist is a trained professional who cares for the nails and feet of clients.

Career Opportunities

The purpose of manicuring and pedicuring is to improve the appearance of the hands, fingernails, feet and toenails. This service, once considered a luxury for wealthy clients, is now used by many well-groomed people. Both men and women receive manicures and pedicures.

The basic manicure consists of washing the patron's hands, removing old polish, filing or shaping the nails, softening and trimming cuticles, applying cream or oil and repolishing the nails, either with regular polishing techniques or French style painting techniques. The pedicure is much the same except you are working on the patron's toenails and feet.

Most manicurists and pedicurists rent workstations in beauty salons. Some choose to work from their homes or make house calls to their clients.

Acrylic nail stylist—This profession requires a cosmetology license in most states and is a good additional service for manicurists to provide to their clients. You can learn the art of nail design by taking classes in acrylic nails, which are available through beauty schools. Once you're licensed, you can rent a station in a busy hair and beauty salon where you will have automatic clientele.

Training
A license to practice cosmetology is required to give professional manicures and pedicures. Contact your State Board of Cosmetology for licensing requirements.

For more information contact

National Association of Accredited Cosmetology Schools
5201 Leesburg Pike, Suite 205
Falls Church, VA 22041
List of accredited cosmetology schools

World International Nail and Beauty Association
1221 North Lake View
Anaheim, CA 92807

Recommended Reading
Finger Tips: Professional Manicurists' Techniques for Beautiful Hands and Feet, Elisa Ferri and Mary-Ellen Siegel, Clarkson Potter, Inc., 1988

Nails, Bobit Publishing, 2512 Artesia Blvd., Redondo Beach, CA 90278, (310) 376-8788—Monthly magazine for the nail care industry

· MASSAGE THERAPIST ·

Career Description
A massage therapist is a professional who is trained to give therapeutic massages to clients.

Career Opportunities
Massage techniques are used worldwide to improve body circulation and skin tone and to help keep the muscles healthy. Massage can also decrease stress and tension. A career as a massage therapist offers flexible hours and high profits for the trained professional.

Many massage therapists have their own practices and work from their own home or office, and some make house calls. Some therapists prefer to work for a doctor or chiropractor.

There are many methods of massage that a massage therapist may practice. Some of these methods include
Swedish Massage—One of the oldest massage techniques and still the most popular. The technique is broken down into four basic strokes: effeurage, petrissage, friction and percussion.
Shiatsu—An Eastern form of massage therapy that uses pressure to calm or stimulate specific accupressure points to balance the body's energy flow.
Sports massage—Used when working with athletes and athletic injuries. A variety of techniques are used for "pre" and "post" athletic events.
Oscillation—A gentle form of massage which uses repetitive back and forth movements to relax the body.
Deep tissue—A form of massage used to release tension and to help heal injuries. It is often incorporated into Swedish massage and sports massage.
Facial massage—Massage can be used to give clients a natural face-lift and reduce signs of aging, and improve the skin's general strength and appearance.

Training

Most states require massage therapists to be licensed. In most cases you will need to obtain classroom training for anywhere from one hundred to five hundred hours (depending on the local requirements) and pass a written exam. Check with your city and county officials.

Training is sometimes available through community college courses, or you may have a massage school in your area. Look in your local yellow pages under "Schools" or contact a local massage therapist to find out where he or she received training.

For more information contact

American Massage Therapy Association
820 Davis Street, Suite 100
Evanston, IL 60201
Information about accredited massage training programs and news about the field, publishers of *Massage Therapy Journal*

The Belavi Institute for Facial Massage
1510 N. Pacific Coast Highway
Laguna Beach, CA 92751
1-800-235-2844
Home-study program to learn facial massage

Bodywork Emporium
414 Broadway
Santa Monica, CA 90401
1-800-822-5348
World's largest supplier of massage therapy supplies, tables, books, vidoes, charts—ask for catalog

Sohnen Moe Associates
3906 W. Ina Road, Suite 200-367

Tuscon, AZ 85741-2295
800-786-4774
Books, computer software and training seminars for massage
therapists about successful business operation and running a
profitable practice

· MEDICAL TRANSCRIPTIONIST ·

Career Description

A medical transcriptionist is a person who translates audio-
tapes from a doctor into written medical records. Medical transcriptionists are used by physicians, hospitals, clinics, insurance
companies and veterinarians.

Career Opportunities

Whenever a patient sees a doctor, the visit is documented.
Most physicians will dictate into a handheld tape recorder or over
the phone into a digital system, reporting on the visit with the
patient. The doctor may speak about why the patient came in for
a visit, what the patient's symptoms are, what the diagnosis is
and the plan to help the patient recover. This dictation must be
translated into a hard-copy format to be placed in the patient's
chart. This written report becomes a part of the patient's medical
records. Each time the patient is seen, the doctor refers to this
record.

Medical transcriptionists must be excellent typists and have
good English skills. Most transcriptionists work freelance for doctor's offices and hospitals and do most of the transcribing at
home.

Training

A medical background is not necessary to enter this career.
Medical transcriptionists must take a course in medical transcrip-

tion, which teaches the basics of human anatomy and physiology. Transcriptionists must also understand medical terminology and be able to translate for doctors with foreign accents. There are training programs available to learn medical transcription.

For more information contact

American Association of Medical Transcription (AAMT)
P.O. Box 576187
Modesto, CA 95357-6187
1-800-982-2182
Professional organization for medical transcriptionists and career information

Northeast Transcripts II, Inc.
14 Crocus Street
Woodbridge, NJ 07095
Home-study training programs to learn medical transcription

· MIDWIFE ·

Career description
Nurse-midwives are trained professionals who assist women during childbirth.

Career Opportunities
Midwives have existed throughout history. Nurse-midwifery was established as a career in America in the 1920s as a response to the high rate of infant and maternal deaths. The first midwife training programs were set up to train these specialty nurses. Today there are more than four thousand certified nurse-midwives working in America, and their numbers increase each year with the growing popularity of birthing centers and home births.

Birthing centers—Birthing centers are alternatives to hospitals where women give birth naturally to babies in a home-like setting. Midwives are present during birth to supervise and assist.

Home births—Midwives are often hired by women who want to have their babies at home. The midwife supervises and assists in home births.

Hospitals—Many hospitals today have a birthing room, which is a section in the maternity ward equipped for childbirth, where women give birth in a home-like setting. Midwives are present to assist during birth.

Training

Nurse-midwives must complete an accredited training program and pass a certification exam before they can begin practicing.

For more information contact

American College of Nurse-Midwives
Education Department
818 Connecticut Avenue NW, Suite 900
Washington, D.C. 20006
List of accredited training programs and career information

Recommended Reading

The Complete Book of Midwifery, Barbara Brennan, C.N.M., and Joan Rattner Heilman, E.P. Dutton & Company, 1977

· MINIATURE MAKER ·

Career Description

A miniature maker is a person who handcrafts miniature replicas of furniture and household items for dollhouses and collectors.

Career Opportunities

Miniature makers create and design small-scale replicas with precision. Collectors and miniature shops buy skillfully crafted miniatures.

Miniatures can be made of furniture, appliances, lamps, rugs, silverware, dishes, food items, clocks, curtains, baskets, flower arrangements, fixtures and every other item that might be found in an ordinary household. Miniatures are made of wood, metal, clay, fabric, glass, plastic and other materials. The possibilities are only limited by the miniature maker's imagination. Miniature makers are creative and always looking for ways to turn ordinary materials into real-looking miniatures.

Miniatures makers usually work from their home workshops or studios.

Once made, miniatures should be packaged individually in clear cellophane bags or in boxes with the maker's name and address. The maker can sell his or her miniatures to specialty shops, at craft shows or by mail order.

Training

There is no training required to become a miniature maker. Practice, patience and a pair of steady hands are helpful.

Recommended Reading

The Complete Book of Making Miniatures, Thelma Newman and Virginia Merrill, Crown Publishers, Inc., 1975

Make Your Own Dolls' House Furniture, Maurice Harper, Guild of Master Craftsmen Publications, Inc., 1995

Nutshell News, Kalmbach Publishing Co., 21027 Crossroads Circle, Waukesha, WI 53187-9951, (414) 796-8776—Monthly magazine for creators and collectors of scale miniatures

· NANNY ·

Career Description

A nanny is a person hired to care for small children, usually in the employer's home. The term "nanny" comes from the Russian word *nyanya,* which means "nursemaid."

Career Opportunities

Many people hire nannies to care for their children as an alternative to day-care centers. In the past, only wealthy families were able to hire nannies, but today nannies are hired by middle-to-upper-class families. Many working couples will hire a nanny to stay at home with their small child.

Nannies are able to give children individualized attention and care, most often in the home.

The duties of a nanny will vary with each assignment and employer. Some nannies are hired solely to care for the family's child or children, while others do additional household tasks such as cleaning, cooking, driving, errands and laundry.

Some nannies for celebrities, prominent families and executives are required to travel with the family.

About 50 percent of nannies live with their employers and the other 50 percent work for the family during the day and live elsewhere. A career as a nanny is perfect for people who love caring for children.

Training

There is no training necessary to become a nanny, although nannies must have child care skills such as feeding, diapering and patience. It is recommended that nannies know CPR and other emergency, lifesaving procedures. A nanny must have good references. Work can be found through domestic agencies who hire nannies, or a nanny can advertise her services in a local paper.

Reccomemded Reading
The Child Care Encyclopedia, Penelope Leach, Knopf, 1983

· NEON SIGN DESIGNER AND REPAIRER ·

Career Description

A neon sign designer designs and creates custom signs made of neon glass. The designer heats and bends the glass to conform to a blueprint pattern. Many restaurants and businesses have flashy neon signs hanging in their shop windows to attract customers.

A neon sign repairer fixes broken and blacked-out neon signs. Over the years, neon signs may begin flickering or cease to light up entirely.

Career Opportunities

Neon signs can be found in every city, and skilled designers and repair technicians are in demand.

This career is an ideal business to operate at home. You can design signs or pick up broken signs and work on them in your home workshop. Simple sign repairs can be done on the spot.

A great way to find repair work is to take an evening walk in your city and look for flickering or broken neon signs. Leave your business card with the owner or manager and offer a free repair estimate. Regular sign companies are also a good source for sign design referrals.

Training

Training is necessary to work with neon signs. Starting as an apprentice for a neon designer is a good way to begin.

For more information contact

ST Publications
407 Gilbert Avenue
Cincinnati, OH 45202
1-800-925-1110
Catalog of books on neon design and repair

Recommended Reading

Signcraft, Signcraft Publishing Company, P.O. Box 06031, Fort Myers, FL 33906, (813) 939-4644—Bimonthly magazine for commercial sign makers

Signs of the Times, ST Publications, 407 Gilbert Avenue, Cincinnati, OH 45202-2285, (513) 421-2050—Monthly trade journal for sign makers

· NEWSLETTER PUBLISHER ·

Career Description

A newsletter publisher is a person who creates and designs newsletters, primarily for businesses and organizations.

Career Opportunities

A newsletter is a great way for people with similar interests, such members of a club or customers of a company, to keep in touch with one another. The best newsletters are informative and attractive to look at. The publisher is hired to design the letter and edit it, and sometimes printing is included in the overall price.

Businesses—Businesses often hire a newsletter publisher to design and write newsletters to go out to their customers, to keep in touch and to generate more business. The publisher gathers information from the business owner or manager and then writes and designs the newsletter. A computer store sends a free newsletter out to its customers twice a year with articles about the latest technology and software, which always brings their customers back to the store.

Organizations and clubs—Newsletter publishers often write newsletters for nonprofit organizations and clubs to keep members up-to-date on current issues, meetings, legislation and informative articles on the particular area of interest.

Independent—Many publishers create their own newsletters that relate to their own interests. One woman started a community newsletter which she publishes monthly. In her newsletter she writes about people and events within the community and interesting articles about local issues. Her newsletter is free, but she charges clients a small fee to place classified help wanted, housing and service ads. Another man created a science-fiction fan newsletter and charges $12 for a yearly subscription. In his newsletter he writes reviews of movies and books, interviews writers and directors in the field and lists upcoming science-fiction conventions. He also has crossword puzzles and trivia sections.

Training

There is no license or official training for newsletter publishers. A publisher must have good writing skills. There are many computer software programs available for publishing newsletters, and there are also books about the subject.

· ORGANIC FARMER ·

Career Description

An organic farmer is a person who grows fruits, vegetables and herbs without using pesticides or premixed chemical fertilizers. Organic farmers rely on natural cycles and fertilizers such as compost.

In recent years, awareness about harmful chemicals in our food has brought about the popularity of organically grown produce. A farmer needs to either own or have access to land on which he or she can grow plants.

Career Opportunities

Produce stand—Fresh produce can be sold at roadside produce stands or at street-fair farmer's markets.

Retail stores—Grocery stores and health food stores will buy your fresh organic produce.

Seeds—You can sell seeds taken from your organically grown plants. Seeds should be dried and packaged in clearly marked envelopes. You can sell them to nurseries, hardware and garden supply stores, or by mail order.

Organic products—You can make edible and delicious condiments from your organic produce, such as jam, jelly, pickles, catsup, mustard, relish and many other things.

Mail order—Dried organic produce can be packaged and sold by mail. Some popular items are nuts, dried fruit and dried herbs.

Training

There is no training necessary to grow produce. There are many books on the subject of organic gardening, cooking and drying fruit and herbs.

For more information contact

The Herb Society of America, Inc.
9019 Kirtland Chardon Rd.
Kirtland, OH 44094

(440) 256-0514
Information about herb growing

The National Agricultural Library
10301 Baltimore Blvd.
Beltsville, MD 20705
Write for a free bibliography about organic farming and gardening

Rodale Publishing Company
33 East Minor Street
Emmaus, PA 18098
Publications about gardening for profit and publisher of *Organic Gardening* magazine

Recommended Reading
The Encyclopedia of Organic Gardening, Rodale Press, 1978

Gardening: The Complete Guide to Growing America's Favorite Fruits and Vegetables, National Gardening Association, Addison-Wesley, 1986

The New Royal Horticulture Society Dictionary of Gardening, Stockton, 1992

The Organic Gardener, Catherine Osgood Foster, Alfred A. Knopf, 1975

· ORGANIZATION CONSULTANT ·

Career Description
An organization consultant is a professional who helps people organize their homes and offices so they get the most out of their space and time.

Career Opportunities

The average person spends sixty hours a year looking for misplaced items. A professional organizer sets up systems to help people reduce clutter and frustration, and teaches clients how to live more efficiently.

Organization consultants work freelance for clients, starting usually with an initial visit where they help reduce clutter and install organizational systems.

Household—Consultants working in the household may reduce clutter and create organized systems in the kitchen, closets, garages, home offices, storage spaces and attics. They may create labeling, filing and storage systems for their clients.

Offices—Consultants working for offices may rearrange furnishings, create storage spaces and organize warehouses and a number of other work spaces. Systems may be created for filing, storage and to make the work area more efficient and organized.

Training

There is no training or licensing required to become an organization consultant. Consultants must be organized and efficient themselves and know how to set up workable systems.

Recommended Reading

Getting Organized, Stephaine Winston, Warner Books, 1991

How to Organize Clutter, Stephanie Culp, Writer's Digest Books, 1990

Organize Your Home, Ronni Eisenberg and Kate Kelly, Hyperion, 1994

Organize Yourself!, Ronni Eisenberg, Macmillan Publishing, 1986

· PARALEGAL ·

Career Description

A paralegal, or lawyer's assistant, is a person who drafts legal documents, does case research and assists the lawyer in trial preparation.

Career Opportunities

Paralegals assist attorneys with research, case preparation, analysis of documents, settling disputes and claims, interviewing witnesses and many other legal duties. Most paralegals work for lawyers in law firms and a few work for state and government agencies such as prosecutors and public defenders. There are four major areas of the legal profession in which paralegals can work: litigation, real estate, probate law and corporate.

Litigation—Litigation paralegals assist attorneys in settling claims and disputes in and out of court. The duties of a paralegal in this field are to research and draft documents, research laws, interview witnesses, keep records, verify information and prepare for trials.

Real estate—Real estate paralegals assist clients who are buying or selling property. The duties of the paralegal in this field would be to draft deeds and contracts, conduct title searches, help buyers obtain loans and assist in closing and foreclosures.

Probate—Probate law involves wills, trusts and estates administration. A paralegal in this field helps people organize their finances and futures. Probate paralegals help attorneys draft wills, create trust funds, value assets and set up accounts.

Corporate—Paralegals in this field work for attorneys in private law firms or within corporations. The duties of a corporate paralegal are to draft documents of incorporation, apply for patents, compile reports, research legislation and prepare annual reports.

Training

Paralegals are not required to be certified or licensed, but to become a paralegal you will need to get training. There are many community colleges and correspondence programs available to teach you what you need to know.

For more information contact

The American Association for Paralegal Education
8826 Santa Fe Drive, Suite 208
Overland Park, KS 66212
(913) 381-4458
List of schools that teach paralegal education

Blackstone School of Law
P.O. Box 701449
Dallas, TX 75370
(972) 418-5141
Paralegal correspondence training programs and career information

The School of Paralegal Studies
6065 Roswell Road, Suite 3118
Atlanta, GA 30328
1-800-223-4542
Paralegal correspondence training programs and career information

Recommended Reading

Finding the Law: A Workbook on Legal Research for Laypersons, Al Coco, William S. Hein, 1986

Find the Law in the Library: A Guide to Legal Research, John Corbin, American Library Association, 1989

Legal Assistant Today, James Publishing, Inc., 3505 Cadillac Avenue, Suite H, Costa Mesa, CA 92626 (714) 755-5450—Bimonthly magazine for paralegals and legal assistants

Legal Research: How to Find and Understand the Law, 2d ed., Stephen Elias, Nolo Press, 1990

· PARAMEDIC ·

Career Description

A paramedic, or emergency medical technician, is a person who gives immediate medical care to injured and ill persons and transports them to medical facilities.

Career Opportunities

Paramedics usually drive ambulances and are dispatched by radio to the scene of emergencies. Their ambulances are equipped to deal with these situations. Paramedics usually work in teams of two and are often the first to arrive at the scene of heart attacks, accidents, childbirths, serious illnesses and poisonings. They administer emergency lifesaving procedures and drive the patient to the nearest hospital. Paramedics often call for help from the police and fire department.

A paramedic can mean the difference between life and death for patients. This is a very challenging and exciting career. A career as a paramedic can be very satisfying if you enjoy helping others through crises.

Paramedics may work for private ambulance companies, fire departments, police departments and hospitals, and usually work a full-time schedule.

Training

A paramedic must have formal training. The certification requirements differ in each state. Classroom work and an internship are required. Check with your state to find out what the certification requirements are. Paramedic training is available at most community colleges or through the fire and police department.

For more information contact your local ambulance companies, hospitals, police and fire departments.

Recommended Reading

9-1-1 magazine, Official Publications, Inc., 18201 Weston Place, Tustin, CA 92680, (714) 544-7776—Bimonthly magazine for emergency response personnel

· PATIO FURNITURE REPAIRER ·

Career Description

Patio furniture made of wood and metal generally is kept outdoors and is exposed to harsh elements such as the sun, rain, snow and wind. Such elements can cause cracking and peeling paint, rotten wood, rusted metal, torn cushions and broken plastic slats. Patio furniture tends to be among the most neglected furnishings of a home.

A patio furniture repairer is a professional who restores old paint, applies new finishes and repairs broken and worn-out seats. This may sound like an odd career, but it has proved quite lucrative for the few professionals who are doing it. While there are many household furniture restorers and refinishers, there are very few people who specialize in outdoor furniture. The field of patio furniture repair is virtually untapped.

Career Opportunities

Home owners—A patio furniture repair person can work locally in his or her own neighborhood. Most homeowners have patio furniture in dire need of repairs. One man in Los Angeles picks up his clients' furniture and takes it home to his garage workshop, where he does the repairs at his leisure.

Hotels and resorts—Nearly every hotel, motel and resort keeps patio furniture available for their guests. Replacement is usually not an option with tight budgets. The worn-out furniture at these establishments needs to be repaired and maintained to keep up a good public image and for their guests' comfort. Rather than hauling all of their furniture to your home workshop, you can do repairs on the spot or in their workshop. Some patio furniture repairers set up maintenance accounts with such clients where they go there year after year and apply new coats of paint and varnish and repair broken items.

Others—Other potential clients might be cruise ships, camps, golf courses and anyplace patio furniture is found.

Training

There is no formal training required for patio furniture repair. You'll need to learn a few basic techniques though, such as sanding, painting, refinishing, upholstering, restrapping and soldering. To learn more about these techniques, you can purchase how-to books about furniture restoration and repair. Go to a patio furniture dealer and get the names of furniture manufacturers. You can write to these companies and get their catalogs of replacement parts.

· PAYROLL ACCOUNTANT ·

Career Description

A payroll accountant is a person who prepares weekly or monthly payrolls for businesses. A payroll accountant maintains payroll records, computes wages and deducts federal and state taxes. Payroll accountants also keep salary records for their clients.

Career Opportunities

Many businesses hire freelance payroll accountants to compute their employees salaries and write paychecks. Preparing a company payroll can be confusing and time-consuming for untrained business owners and bookkeepers. Many companies, both large and small, regularly hire an outside service that will handle their payroll with competence and speed.

Most payroll accountants have several clients at one time, which keeps them working full-time. Businesses who use payroll accountants usually drop off the payroll data to the accountant's home or office a day or two before the checks are to be dispersed to employees. The payroll accountant computes the employees' salaries, makes the proper deductions, writes and prints the payroll checks and usually delivers them to clients on Fridays.

A career as a payroll accountant is ideal for those who want to work at home.

Training

Payroll accountants must be trained specifically in bookkeeping and payroll accounting. They must know the current state and federal tax deductions. You can take courses offered at community colleges or enroll in a home-study program. The training is usually six months to one year.

For more information contact

At Home Professions
2001 Lowe Street
Fort Collins, CO 80525
(303) 225-6300
Correspondence course on payroll accounting

National Career Institute
2021 West Montrose Avenue

Chicago, IL 60618
Correspondence course on payroll accounting

• PEDORTHIST •

Career Description

A pedorthist is a designer, manufacturer and modifier of shoes to alleviate foot problems caused by disease, injury or overuse. A pedorthist makes specialized shoes to relieve or accommodate foot problems on a temporary or permanent basis.

Over the course of a lifetime, some people experience foot problems that call for customized footwear to help with everything from minor discomforts such as calluses to major injuries and physical deformities.

A pedorthist customizes and modifies prescription shoes as described in the doctor's diagnosis for the patient. Pedorthists are an important part of the medical team. They can help reduce hospitalization and surgery in some cases.

Career Opportunities

Many pedorthists have their own private practices and work by appointment, filling prescriptions from doctors. Other pedorthists work for footwear manufacturers.

Training

To become a board-certified pedorthist (C.Ped.), you must study pedorthics, obtain practical experience and pass a national examination in the field. Currently, to qualify to take the examination, you must have 120 hours of formal training in pedorthics.

For more information contact

Pedorthic Footwear Association
9861 Broken Land Parkway, Suite 255
Columbia, MD 21046-1151
(410) 381-7278
Information about careers in pedorthics and how to become
certified

· PERFUMER ·

Career Description

A perfumer is a person who designs and creates fragrances,
perfumes and colognes. Perfumers, or "noses," are held in the
highest esteem in the perfume industry. They make the final decisions as to whether or not a fragrance will be marketed.

Perfume has been a part of society since the ancient Egyptians
first discovered how to extract fragrant essential oils from flowers
and plants. The great perfumers of eighteenth-century France re-
fined and developed the art of perfumery as we know it today.

Perfumery is a very secretive business and formulas are well
guarded by their creators. It has been said that a truly good perfume will improve with age like a fine wine. It can be tricky to
make a perfume that will smell as good in one year as it did when
it was created. Each perfume consists of three parts: the top note,
the middle note and the bottom note. The top note is the first
scent that is smelled when the bottle is opened and the perfume
put on the skin. The middle note is the scent that stays on the
skin, layered over the bottom note, which is the final scent that
lasts for several hours.

Career Opportunities

Successful perfumers can become very wealthy if their scent
catches on and becomes popular. A tiny, one-ounce bottle of good

perfume can retail for hundreds of dollars. Perfumers can develop new scents for laboratories, or they can create, market and sell their own perfumes.

Training

There are a few schools that teach the basics of perfumery, but real success depends upon the creativity and the nose of the perfumer. Most perfumers start out as apprentices for established perfumers. A background and understanding of organic chemistry is helpful and recommended for new perfumers to understand the relationship between structure and odor, but not entirely necessary.

I interviewed a famous perfumer who admitted that he had never had any formal training throughout his career and learned the trade by working as an assistant to another perfumer. He credits his success to his sense of smell and creativity. Perfumers must have an excellent sense of smell.

For more information contact

The Fragrance Foundation
145 East 32nd Street
New York, NY 10016
(212) 725-2755
List of schools offering perfumery courses, industry books, newsletters and information about perfumery and fragrance marketing

Victorian Essence
P.O. Box 1220
Arcadia, CA 91077
888-446-5455
Perfume making supplies and formula books

Recommended Reading

Formulary of Perfume and Cosmetics, R. M. Gattefosse, Chemical Publishing, 1959—Eighteenth-century French perfume and toiletry formulas translated into English

Perfumes, Potions & Fanciful Formulas—Victorian Press, Kelly Reno, 1997—Formulas for perfume, cologne, oils, powders and other toiletries

· PERSONAL FITNESS TRAINER ·

Career Description

A personal fitness trainer is a person who helps others attain their fitness goals through personalized exercise instruction.

Trainers are hired by clients to lose weight, tone muscles and to help them develop a training routine. Athletes and celebrities also hire personal fitness trainers.

Career Opportunities

Personal fitness trainers deliver private training sessions to their clients at the client's home or at a gym. Most trainers see their clients several times a week until the client has reached his or her fitness goals. Celebrities, executives and affluent people commonly hire trainers.

Instructors may teach aerobics, weight training, endurance, muscle toning, bodybuilding, proper use of exercise equipment and self-defense training.

Keeping your clients motivated is important and probably one of the primary reasons they hired you.

Training

Personal fitness trainers must know how to teach fitness routines to others at graduated levels. Some states require that trainers have a license.

Recommended Reading

American Fitness, 15250 Ventura Blvd., Suite 200, Sherman Oaks, CA 91403, (818) 905-0040—Bimonthly magazine covering fitness, exercise and nutrition

Idea Today, The International Association of Fitness Professionals, 6190 Cornerstone Court E., Suite 204, San Diego, CA 92121, (619) 535-8979—Magazine for personal fitness trainers

· PHOTOGRAPHER ·

Career Description

A freelance photographer is a professional who photographs people and events. There are many work opportunities for photographers.

Photographers need to own a high-quality camera and know how to use lighting and backgrounds to make subjects look their best. Photographers are creative and artistic.

Career Opportunities

Event photography—Photographers are hired to cover important events that their clients want to capture on film. Common events that photographers cover are weddings, anniversaries, parties, sporting events and news events.

Still photography—Still photographers usually work in studios and take photographs of still items. They are often hired by advertising companies to take photos of products.

Portraits—A portrait photographer usually works in a studio and photographs family portraits, wedding albums, baby pictures, pets and headshots for actors and actresses.

Fashion—Fashion photographers photograph fashion shows and models and know how to make the subject's clothing look its best. Fashion photographers usually work with makeup and hair artists to make the models look their best. Fashion photography is done in a studio or on location. No two ways to break into the business are the same. One amateur photographer began photographing London "street fashion" and used the photos to create a small, trendy magazine. The photographer is now very popular and receiving high-paying assignments.

Art—Art photographers take photos of beautiful and interesting items, scenery and people. These photos are then sold to collectors or used in calendars, magazines or coffee table books. The famous photographer Ansel Adams was an art photographer.

Photojournalist—Photojournalists take photographs of interesting places, people and events and write stories to go along with their pictures. These photos and stories are sold to magazines, newspapers and periodicals. For more information read the entry in this book on the Freelance Reporter.

Training

Photographers can get started in many ways. First, they must know how to take good photographs, which they can learn by taking courses in photography available at nearly every community college. Some new photographers work as interns or assistants in studios or for newspapers. Other photographers begin by collecting their photos in a book to show samples of their work to clients. There is no one way to enter the field. Talent, creativity and ambition are the determining factors of a photographer's career.

For more information contact

The Seattle Filmworks Photography School
P.O. Box 34725
Seattle, WA 98124-9902
(206) 283-9074
Photography correspondence courses

Recommended Reading

The Artist's Market, Writer's Digest Books, updated yearly This book contain lists of companies and publishers that hire artists and buy photographs, and information on how to break in and how to submit work

Portfolio, Institute for Photographic Excellence, P.O. Box 3994, Walnut Creek, CA 94598—Bimonthly journal covering photography

Professional Photographer, Professional Photographers of America, Inc., 1090 Executive Way, Des Plaines, IL 60018-1587—Monthly magazine for professional portrait, wedding, commercial and industrial photographers

The Rangefinder, 1312 Lincoln Blvd., Santa Monica, CA 90406—Monthly magazine for professional photographers

· PICTURE FRAMER ·

Career Description

A picture framer is a professional who mounts artwork and other important documents in picture frames.

Career Opportunities

Picture framers are hired by clients to preserve and display many art items, such as oil paintings, watercolor paintings, photographs and drawings. Other important documents that a framer might frame are diplomas, birth certificates, marriage certificates, awards and magazine and newspaper articles.

The framer helps clients choose the right frame and matting for the project. Matting is stiff paper that is available in many colors, patterns and textures. It is used to border the framed item.

Some framed pictures have two or three layers of matting in different colors to enhance pictures. Framers also cut pieces of glass to fit the frame properly.

Framers can be hired to put together collages in framing boxes, and to frame needlepoint and cross-stitching work and other items that clients want to display and preserve.

Most framers own their own framing businesses, but some work freelance for painters, photographers and other artists.

Training

Picture framing can be learned by taking courses offered at community colleges and art schools. Some framers start out working as an apprentice for an established framer to learn the business. There are also books available about picture framing which can be studied and then practiced.

For more information contact

Professional Picture Framers Association (PPFA)
4305 Sarellen Road
Richmond, VA 23231
(804) 226-0430
Training seminars and career information for picture framers

Recommended Reading
Picture Framing, Fay Boon, Chartwell Books, 1995

Suitable for Framing: The Floral Garden, and *Suitable for Framing: Fruits of the Earth*, Gramercy Park Books—How to mat and frame pictures, with artwork to practice with

· PILOT ·

Career Description

Commercial pilots are highly trained professionals who fly both small and large aircrafts to transport passengers and cargo. Experienced pilots may also obtain a special license to teach flying lessons to students.

Most pilots work freelance transporting passengers on business and vacation, or they may be hired by a large corporation to transport executives, employees and cargo. Many people hire pilots if they need to get someplace quickly or need to get to a remote location where there is only a small airport that can't handle the traffic of commercial airlines. A career as a pilot is both exciting and challenging.

Career Opportunities

Pilot for hire—This type of pilot transports individuals and groups to their destinations for vacation and business trips. Reservations are usually made in advance with the pilot.

Cargo transportation—Pilots are often hired to fly cargo from one location to another.

Burial at sea—Pilots are often hired by the family of a deceased person to drop the ashes of their loved one over a particular location or over the sea.

Scenic tours—Pilots fly tourists over scenic locations to get an aerial view. Such tours are popular at the Grand Canyon, Niagara Falls and other popular tourist attractions.

Aerial advertising—Pilots are hired by businesses to fly advertising banners over towns and at big events. Some pilots use smoke writing to write giant messages in the sky.

Fish spotting—Pilots are hired by fishing companies to fly over the ocean or lakes to spot large schools of fish visible from the air. The pilot then radios the location of the fish and the fishing boats are sent in.

Patrol—Big corporations such as oil and electricity companies hire pilots to fly over pipelines and electrical lines. The pilot flies along the underwater lines with a technician from the company who is geared with testing equipment to check for leaks and other problems.

TV/radio traffic reports/weather—Pilots often work for TV and radio stations and report on the traffic and weather forecasts.

Airplane delivery—Pilots are hired by airplane manufacturers, corporations and individuals to deliver airplanes to destinations worldwide. It is less expensive to have a pilot fly a new plane to its destination than to take it apart and ship it in pieces.

Flight instruction—A licensed pilot can teach others to fly.

Search and rescue—Pilots are hired by counties and states to conduct searches for missing persons in remote areas not accessible by foot, such as mountainous areas. Other counties hire pilots to look for fires.

Helicopters—Many of the above careers may be done by a helicopter pilot. A pilot must obtain a special license to operate helicopters.

Training

To become a commercial pilot, the Federal Aviation Association requires that you study airplanes as a theoretical subject and pass written and oral exams.

A pilot must first obtain a pilot's license, which requires about forty flight hours (twenty with a flying instructor and twenty flying solo). After pilots have obtained their license, they may then complete additional training programs and flight hours to increase their rank to commercial pilot.

Commercial pilots must have at least 250 total flight hours and pass another set of exams. Commercial pilots usually learn how to fly multi-engine aircraft. They are allowed to transport passengers and cargo for a fee. To fly a plane over 12,500 pounds or an aircraft with jet engines, a pilot must obtain a license to operate the particular aircraft that he or she will be flying.

Nearly every airport, large and small, has a flying school on its grounds. Call up your local airport to find out about requirements and how to get started.

For more information contact

Aviation Supplies & Academics, Inc.
6001 Sixth Avenue South
Seattle, WA 98108-3307
Pilot training manuals and test preparation materials, write for book catalog

Federal Aviation Association/Department of Transportation
Aviation Careers Division
AMH-300
P.O. Box 25082
Oklahoma City, OK 73125
Write for free aviation career information

King Aviation Centers
16644 Roscoe Blvd.
Van Nuys, CA 91406
1-800-273-4686
Flight instruction and career information

· PRIVATE INVESTIGATOR ·

Career Description
An investigator conducts data searches and surveillances for the purpose of determining activities, truthfulness, present

whereabouts, associations and affiliations of various subjects. Using still and video cameras, an investigator can document a person's activities, damage to vehicles and property, personal injuries and accident-scene reconstruction.

Investigators conduct searches for assets; compile background reports using various sources and methods that incorporate interviews, document research, undercover contact, surveillance and shadowing; find witnesses and others who don't want to be found; take photographs; locate missing evidence; obtain statements; survey jurors; identify conflicts of interest and verify undesirable conduct. Investigators also conduct searches of public records and computer databases.

Private investigators work freelance for individuals who are seeking the truth about some matter.

Career Opportunities

Missing persons—An investigator may be hired by an individual to locate a person who is missing.

Skip Tracer—An investigator who, using public and private sources, telephone interviewing techniques and other methods, locates companies and individuals who have moved or are hiding their whereabouts. A skip tracer might also compile other background information on individuals and companies who are the subject of an investigation and, in some cases, locate assets in collection matters.

Record Searcher—An investigator who searches public records in city, county, state and federal jurisdictions; briefs, court records and other documents; and utilizes computers databases to access information about a suspect.

Shadowing surveillance—An investigator may secretly "shadow" or follow suspects to find out about their activities, whereabouts, acquaintances and affiliations. A good example of a job would be a man who hires an investigator to follow his wife when he believes she is having an affair.

Training

Your state may require private investigators to have a license, which is obtained by taking a test. Training is available for this profession.

For more information contact

National Association of Legal Investigators
P.O. Box 3254
Alton, IL 62002
1-800-266-6254
Investigator certification

The Nick Harris Detective Academy
16917 Enadia Way
Van Nuys, CA 91406
1-800-642-5427

West Coast Detective Academy
5113 Lankershim Blvd.
North Hollywood, CA 91601
1-800-752-5555

Recommended Reading

How to Find Almost Anyone, Anywhere, Norma Mott Tillman, Rutledge Hill Press, 1994

How to Find Anyone Anywhere, Ralph Thomas, Thomas Publications, 1991

You, Too, Can Find Anybody, Joseph J. Culligan, Hallmark Press, Inc., 1995

· PRIVATE LABEL COSMETICS SALESPERSON ·

Career Description

Private label cosmetics are products made by a cosmetic manufacturer and sold to private individuals under the individual's company name. These products are then sold to wholesalers and retailers by the person who ordered them.

Career Opportunities

Most of the cosmetic products that you find in stores, from shampoos and conditioners to hairsprays and lotions, were made by a private label laboratory. Private label laboratories specialize in making cosmetics and selling custom orders to clients. For example, if you wanted to make your own line of peach-scented bubble bath, you could take your ideas to a private label manufacturer and they would develop your recipe, help you choose bottles and caps, word your labels and fill the bottles for you. Manufacturers also make products such as nail polish, soap, toothpaste, makeup and a wide variety of other cosmetics.

People who have their own lines of cosmetics made are able to resell their products to wholesalers and retailers and make from $1 to $5 profit on each item. The markup on cosmetic products is one of the highest around.

Cosmetic products can be sold to drugstores, discount stores, boutiques, beauty salons, grocery stores, by mail order and to virtually anyplace cosmetic products are sold. New products can also be taken to cosmetic trade shows, where cosmetic buyers for stores come to place orders.

The cost of private label manufacturing varies, but generally, a bottle of a completed product will cost you from 35¢ to $1.95

per bottle, depending on the quantity you order. Some private label manufacturers have minimum orders of 10,000 and some will handle small runs of 1,500 units. Some private label manufacturers will include the cost of product liability insurance with your order.

To be successful, you'll need to come up with a new, interesting and aesthetic product that fills a need. There is a lot of competition in this field.

A woman in Pasadena had her own line of shampoo made by a private label manufacturer. She had always been allergic to strong perfumes in shampoos and had a hard time finding a good unscented shampoo. After completing a marketing research survey, she discovered that other people shared her feelings about scented shampoo. She went to a private label laboratory and had her own line of unscented shampoo manufactured. She set up accounts with many stores in her area and reordered bottles from the laboratory as needed to fill her orders. The woman pays the laboratory 92¢ per bottle and sells her product wholesale for $4.50 and retail for $8.00.

This career can make you a lot of money if you're able to dream up a new product and market it cleverly. You will need initial money to invest in your first order, ranging from $1,500 on up.

Training

There is no training necessary to get started in this career. The specialists at the laboratories will formulate safe recipes for you. It is advised that you conduct a marketing research survey before you have your new product manufactured, to make sure that there is a need for it. It is also advised that you contact an attorney to find out about product liability insurance. You want to ensure that you are fully covered.

Call a few private label cosmetic laboratories and find out what type of products they manufacture and their prices. To find a private label manufacturer, look in the business-to-business yellow pages under "Cosmetic Manufacturers."

• PROMOTIONAL ITEMS DISTRIBUTOR •

Career Description

A promotional items distributor sells promotional items to businesses and organizations to help them generate more business.

Businesses of all types, large and small, need to let potential customers know that they exist. One of the best ways to do this is by advertising through promotional items. By becoming a promotional items distributor, you can help these businesses grow (and make a great living). Every year businesses and organizations spend millions of dollars on promotional items imprinted with their name or logo, such as key chains, pens, notepads, magnets, bags, coffee cups and many others.

The manufacturers of these items hire freelance representatives to sell their products to businesses and organizations, who then personalize them to promote their company or group.

Career Opportunities

This career can be done successfully in any city or state, wherever there are businesses that are potential clients.

Training

There is no training necessary to start this career. To get started right away, look in your local phone book under "Advertising" or "Advertising Specialties" and you'll find several companies that sell promotional items.

Make an appointment to see the owner of a company and let him or her know that you'd like to work as an independent representative. The owner will be overjoyed and will send you off with a catalog and a bag full of samples. You then can contact businesses and organizations (personal visits are best) and show them your product line. Help the business decide what items would work best for them and take your first order back to the "advertising specialty" shop.

When pricing, make sure to add on your fee. For example, if personalized coffee cups cost $1.00 to manufacture, charge $1.05 each and keep the difference as your pay. You don't have to be a representative for only one company. You may work freelance for several promotional items manufacturers. This will allow you to offer a large and competitively priced product line to your clients.

· PROPERTY APPRAISER ·

Career Description

Property appraisers use their knowledge and expertise to determine the value of residential and commercial real estate. Appraisers gather and analyze data and typically prepare written reports to document their reports and conclusions.

Career Opportunities

Appraisers may be hired to appraise a variety of property types, including single-family homes, apartment buildings, shopping centers, office buildings, factories, farms and many others. People who hire property appraisers use the appraiser's opinion to help them make decisions. Appraisers may be hired in many situations, such as buying and selling, negotiating price, before lenders lend money, before insurance companies issue a policy, for tax assessment and when required by city, county and government agencies. Appraisers are needed whenever real estate is sold, mortgaged, taxed, developed and insured.

Most property appraisers have their own businesses and appraise property for clients. Some appraisers work for private appraisal firms or real estate companies. Appraisers are out in the field most of the time inspecting property and researching records.

Training

Property appraisers spend much of their time conducting research. Appraisers must be able to search public records; read blueprints; understand financing, architecture and construction and be able to write and communicate clearly.

Most states require property appraisers to become certified or licensed. Contact your state's regulatory agency for specific requirements.

For more information contact

American Bankers Association
Attention: Customer Service Center
1120 Connecticut Avenue NW.
Washington, D.C. 20036
800-338-0626
Home-study correspondence course in real estate appraisal

Appraisal Institute
875 North Michigan Avenue, Suite 2400
Chicago, IL 60611
(312) 335-4100
Organization for real estate appraisers

H2 Company
315 Whitney Avenue
New Haven, CT 06511
(203) 562-3159
Books, forms, correspondence courses about real estate appraisal

National Association of Real Estate Appraisers
1224 N. Nokomis
Alexandria, MN 56308
(320) 763-7626
Professional organization for real estate appraisers

· PUBLICIST ·

Career Description
A publicist is a person who generates media interest in a client and his or her works. Many celebrities, authors and people in the public eye hire a publicist to make their works known to the general public.

Career Opportunities
Publicists establish connections to people who work in the different media, such as television, radio and print, and let their contacts know about their clients and/or their works. The publicist communicates about his or her clients in such a way that the media see the clients to be newsworthy and thus release favorable press about the client. Publicists usually charge clients per campaign.

Celebrities—Many celebrities and people in the public eye, including politicians and other prominent figures, hire publicists to improve their image, promote a new project or campaign and to gain attention. Publicists often write and release press releases and stories about celebrities that are picked up and broadcast on TV or radio, or printed in newspapers or magazines.
Businesses and organizations—Businesses often hire publicists to generate more business or to promote a new product. Publicists can create goodwill events to gain press for their business clients.
Recently, a small business hired a publicist who suggested that

the company sponsor a local poetry contest. This contest resulted in local news appearances and newspaper articles about the owner, his business and of course the contest, and generated much new business. Another business launched their new product by hiring a publicist who wrote a press release and sent out samples to the local media, which created a demand for the new product.

Authors—Many book authors and their publishers hire publicists to book TV, radio and news interviews. Publicists also set up book tours for authors.

Damage control—Publicists are often hired by individuals and businesses who have had a rash of bad press and want to improve their public image. The publicist creates goodwill campaigns for the client and concentrates on getting favorable press by writing stories or holding a press conference to point out the positive aspects of the person.

Recommended Reading

Effective Public Relations, Scott M. Cutlipp, Prentice Hall, 1985

Gebbie Press Directory, Gebbie Press, annual publication listing all media sources

Handbook for Public Relations Writing, Thomas Bivens, NTC Business Books, 1995

Lesly's Public Relations Handbook, Philip Lesly, Prentice Hall, 1983

Public Relations Workbook, Raymond Simon and Joseph M. Zappala, NTC Publishing Group, 1996

· REAL ESTATE AGENT ·

Career Description

A real estate agent is a person who represents clients who are buying or selling property.

Career Opportunities

The real estate market is booming, which creates many opportunities for real estate agents.

Real estate agents must work for a broker. A broker is a person who is licensed to have other agents working for him or her and usually operates an office or franchise. Real estate agents choose the broker they wish to work for. Brokers take a percentage of the agent's commission on homes sold or bought. Working with a broker provides the agent with clients, advertising and other benefits. Some agents work out of the broker's office, while others work from their homes.

Real estate agents should join their city or county real estate board. Becoming a member of the local board gives the agent access to multiple listing books (lists of all homes for sale in the area) and access to electronic keys, which are used by agents to open lock boxes on homes.

Selling homes—When an agent has a client that wants to sell a home, the agent puts together a property profile, which is done by pulling the property title from a title company, which is a public record. The title will tell the agent when the home was built, what liens are on the property, if any, easements (when the owner has given another person rights to use the property), how much the property was purchased for and who the rightful owner is. The agent can then gather information about other similar properties to determine the fair market value of the property. The agent signs a listing agreement with the client and submits the listing in the local listing directory. The agent usually puts up a "for sale" sign in the yard and may also advertise the property in newspapers, magazines or by holding an open house. When someone wants to buy the property and has made an acceptable offer, the agent must go through an escrow company, which handles the financial transactions; files the new deed; pays off the seller, agent and any taxes and makes sure that all work or repairs specified are completed. When escrow closes, the agent is paid a commission, which is split with his or her broker.

Buying homes—Real estate agents help clients buy homes. When a new client comes to an agent, the agent will prequalify the buyer. Prequalifying is when the agent finds out how much money the client wants to spend, what type of home he or she wishes to buy, what neighborhood, what style, how much down payment is available and how the client's credit is. The agent usually goes through the listing books and picks out several properties to show the client. When the client finds a property he or she likes, the agent helps the client make a fair offer. If the offer is accepted and escrow closes, the agent is paid a commission, which is split with the broker.

Training

Real estate agents in all states must be licensed. Most new agents take a general course in real estate practice through a real estate school and then may take their state licensing exam. Call your State Board of Real Estate for licensing requirements and a list of approved schools. There are also courses available to help new agents pass the licensing test. Once agents are licensed, they must continue to renew their license by taking continuing education classes.

For more information contact

The National Association of Realtors
430 North Michigan Avenue
Chicago, IL 60611

1-800-874-6500
Information about careers in real estate

Recommended Reading
Barron's Dictionary of Real Estate Terms, 3rd ed., Barron
Publishing, 1993

· REFLEXOLOGIST ·

Career Description

Reflexology is a reflex acupressure technique designed specifically for the feet. This form of massage, while localized at the feet, can be beneficial to the entire body. This technique was developed by the Chinese to restore a healthy energy flow through the body. The technique is based on the belief that each nerve ending in the foot is connected by a pathway to a specific organ or system of the body. Stimulating these nerve endings properly can help with many health problems.

A reflexologist practices these massage techniques to help clients relax, stimulate circulation, increase energy, relieve stress and even for weight loss.

Career Opportunities

Reflexology is relatively new to the United States and is growing in popularity, thus creating a demand for professional reflexologists. Most reflexologists have their own private practices.

Training

At this time, there are no licensing requirements for reflexologists, although most professionals have gone through a training program to learn the art. Some cities classify reflexology under massage and you may be required to obtain certification. See the Massage Therapist entry for more information.

For more information contact

The American Massage Therapy Association
820 Davis Street, Suite 100
Evanston, IL 60201
Write for a list of accredited training schools

International Institute of Reflexology
P.O. Box 12642
St. Petersburg, FL 33733
(727) 343-4811
Nationwide training programs, books, charts and information
about reflexology

· REPORTER ·

Career Description

A freelance reporter is a person who writes about people, issues and events for a publication such as a newspaper or magazine.

Career Opportunities

Stories and reports covered can be fictional, such as, or non-
fictional, such as investigative reports; coverage of events; stories
about people, travel and issues.

Newspapers—Daily and weekly newspapers accept and publish
articles from freelance reporters and writers. Some pay and others
do not. Contact the newspapers in your area.
Fashion and women—Nearly every major fashion and women's
magazine publishes articles written by freelance reporters and
writers on subjects such as fashion, beauty, decorating and cooking, and short stories as well.

Other publications—There are many specialized publications for business and industry that publish technical articles written by freelance reporters. These publications cover law, farming, computers, sales, insurance, automobiles and hundreds of other subjects.

To get started as a freelance reporter, get the names and addresses of publications you'd like to write articles for. Send a letter to the managing editor asking for his or her story guidelines and how much the publication pays. Other reporters sell stories to news wire services. Wire services make stories available for all newspapers across the country to pick up.

Training

There is no formal training required to become a freelance reporter. Reporters must have good writing skills and the ability to cover stories in a creative and fresh manner.

Recommended Reading

The Associated Press Stylebook and Libel Manual, 6th ed., Addison-Wesley Publishing Company, 1996

Gebbie Press Directory, Gebbie Press—Annual publication listing all media sources

The Writer's Market, Writer's Digest Books, updated yearly— Complete listings for magazine publishers

· RÉSUMÉ WRITER ·

Career Description

A résumé writer is a person who helps others create and design résumés to help them get the jobs they want.

Career Opportunities

With more layoffs and fewer jobs, people are finding themselves suddenly unemployed. With more people out of work, the job marketplace becomes crowded and competitive. Other people are looking to change jobs or switch careers.

Résumé writers give their clients the cutting edge by providing a professional and well-written résumé. A résumé reflects a person's image and ability and often makes the difference between getting interviewed and hired by potential employers and not making it through the door. A good résumé writer is creative and knows how to promote his or her clients through their résumés. Résumé writers must also have a good understanding of the English language.

Most résumé writers meet with their clients and find out what sort of experience, education, skills, talents and abilities they have. They then find out what type of job their client is looking for and slant the résumé toward the client's career goals. Most résumé writers work in their home offices and use computers.

Training

There is no training necessary to write résumés for others. There are many reference books about résumé writing available at bookstores and libraries.

Recommended Reading

The New Perfect Résumé, Tom Jackson and Ellen Jackson, Doubleday, 1996

Power Résumés, Ron Tepper, John Wiley & Sons, 1989

The Résumé Handbook, Arthur D. Rosenberg and David Hizer, Adams Media Corp., 1996

Résumé Writing, Burdette E. Bostwock, John Wiley & Sons, Inc., 1990

· SHOE REPAIRER ·

Career Description

A shoe repairer is a skilled individual who can repair shoes and handbags. Repairers must know how to fix heels, dye leather, remove and replace soles, stretch leather and repair tears.

Career Opportunities

Most shoe repairers operate their own shops.

Shoe repair—Most shoes are made of leather. Over time shoes need new soles, heels repaired and rips mended. Many people choose to have their shoes repaired rather than replaced. A shoe repairer can repair shoes and knows how to dye leather to match the original color.

Handbags—Leather handbags need repairs from time to time, and people often take their bags to a shoe repairer. Straps break, linings need to be replaced, rips require mending and dyeing and other treatments need to be done.

Training

Most shoe repairers learn the trade by working as apprentices in a repair shop. There are also many books about the subject which can be found in libraries. Shoe repairers must be skilled.

For more information contact

Small Business Administration
U.S. Government Printing Office
Washington, D.C. 20402

Ask for publication *Starting and Managing a Small Shoe Service Shop*

Recommended Reading
Shoe Repairing, Henry Karg, The Bruce Publishing Company, 1965

Shoe Service, SSIA Corporation, 5024-R Campbell Blvd., Baltimore, MD 21236, (410) 931-8100—Monthly magazine for shoe repairers

· SILK FARMER ·

Career Description
A silk farmer is a person who raises silkworms and processes silk.

Career Opportunities
Raw silk comes from the cocoons of silkworms. Today, a handful of people in the United States are raising silkworms and processing their own silk. This ancient industry originated in China around 1523 B.C. under the Shang Dynasty. The Chinese guarded the secrets of the art until A.D. 300, when the Japanese acquired the technology. Later, the technology spread across Europe and other parts of the world. The first silk mill in the United States was established in 1810.

Hand-processed silk is still today considered very valuable and is often used to create special gowns and tapestries. Raw silk is not imported into the United States anymore, only processed silk.

Most silkworm growers start by purchasing a small amount of silkworm eggs. The eggs are placed in boxes where the worms hatch. The hatched silkworms must be fed fresh mulberry leaves every few hours. The worms eat leaves for a month or so and then begin spinning silk cocoons. The silkworms hatch into moths and the silk cocoons can then be processed and spun into silk thread. The hatched moths will lay more eggs, which can be stored in the refrigerator and hatched at a later date.

Training

There is no training required to become a silk farmer. Beginners wishing to get into this profession should read about the subject and start off with a small silkworm farm their first year to get the hang of it. If you're going to raise silkworms, you'll need to have access to mulberry trees, as that's the only food source silkworms will do well on. You will also need to have space for their boxes, in a garage or other out-of-the-way place. For information on spinning silk, see the entry in this book for Spinster.

Recommended Reading

Culture of the Mulberry Silkworm, Henrietta A. Kelly, United States Department of Agriculture, Division of Entomology, bulletin no. 39, new series, 1903

Handbook of Silkworm Rearing: Agriculture Technique Manual, Japan's Ministry of Agriculture and Forestry, International Cooperation Section, 1972

A Silk Worker's Notebook, Cheryl Kolander, Interweave Press, 201 East 4th Street, Loveland, CO 80537, 1-800-645-3675

Spin-off Magazine, Summer 1994 issue, Interweave Press, 201 East 4th Street, Loveland, CO 80537, 1-800-645-3675—This issue is about raising silkworms.

Utah History Quarterly 46, no. 4 (1978): pgs. 376–396, "The Finest of Fabrics: Mormon Women and the Silk Industry," Chris Rigby Arrington

· SPINSTER ·

Career Description

A spinster or spinner is a person who makes yarn by twisting and winding wool, cotton and other natural fibers into yarn on a spinning wheel.

Career Opportunities

Pioneer women used to spin their own yarn using wooden spinning wheels. Today many people spin yarn as a career using the old-fashioned wooden spinning wheels or the modern electric version.

Hand-spun yarn made from natural fibers is making a big comeback and can bring the spinster big bucks per ball! Wool and angora fibers are used to make the most expensive yarns. Spinsters usually obtain raw wool fibers from farmers or from fiber suppliers. Some spinsters raise their own angora rabbits or other animals and weave their fur into beautiful and pricey yarn. Rabbits tend to multiply quickly, and a couple of them can quickly turn into large families that will keep the spinster busy for years. Cotton can also be spun into beautiful yarn.

Many spinsters color their own fibers in beautiful shades using natural plant dyes which increases the value of their yarn.

Homespun yarn can be sold to yarn shops, fabric stores, knitters, crocheters or by mail order.

For more information contact

The Yarn Barn
930 Massachusetts St.
Lawrence, KS 66044
1-800-468-0035
Spinning wheels, spinning supplies, fiber, dyes and how-to books, ask for catalog

Recommended Reading

Hands On Spinning, Lee Raven, Interweave Press, 1997

In Sheep's Clothing: A Handspinner's Guide to Wool, Nola Fourniert, Interweave Press, 1995

Shuttle, Spindle & Dyepot, 120 Mountain Road, Bloomfield, CT 06002—Magazine covering spinning and dyeing

Spin-Off, Interweave Press, 201 East 4th Street, Loveland, CO 80537, (303) 669-7672—Quarterly magazine covering handspinning, dyeing, techniques and projects for using handspun fibers

· SPRINKLER TECHNICIAN ·

Career Description

A sprinkler technician is a person who installs, repairs and maintains outdoor watering systems for home owners and businesses.

Career Opportunities

About 50 percent of the lawns in the country have sprinkler systems. This is good news for anyone considering a career as a sprinkler technician, because the 50 percent that have existing systems need those to be maintained and repaired, while the other 50 percent are potential customers for new installation.

With many drought-prone areas across the country and soaring water prices, many home owners and businesses are installing energy-efficient systems that are designed to conserve water and minimize energy waste. Sprinkler systems raise the value of property, replacing frustrating and wasteful hose watering and hose sprinklers.

Sprinkler technicians design the layout of new sprinkler systems, install them, and repair old systems. A sprinkler technician in California makes his living offering customers a "sprinkler tune-up," which is a program to maintain the system and make sure that the water is distributed efficiently. Landscapers and contractors are a good source of referrals for sprinkler technicians.

Training

Sprinkler technicians must be trained. Some states may require sprinkler technicians to be licensed contractors. Call your State Contractors Board to find out about licensing requirements.

Some technicians learn the trade by apprenticing for an established technician. There is also training available through vocational schools and home-study programs.

For more information contact

Builder's Books, Inc.
8001 Canoga Avenue
Canoga Park, CA 91304
1-800-273-7375
Books about sprinkler systems and landscape design, ask for catalog

Prentice Hall
Wheels of Learning—Sprinkler Fitter Program
200 Old Tappan Road
Old Tappan, NJ 07675
1-800-922-0579
Sprinkler technician training manuals

Recommended Reading
Lawn Sprinklers, a Do-It-Yourself Guide, Richard L. Austin, TAB Books, 1990

· STAINED GLASS ARTIST ·

Career Description

A stained glass artist creates and designs windows, lamps, sun catchers, panels and other works of art with colored glass and metal.

Career Opportunities

Churches and cathedrals are best known for their dazzling stained glass murals and windows. Many churches still hire stained glass artists to create beautiful windows. Stained glass is also commonly found in homes—in the windows, inlaid into doors and as beautiful sun catchers and panels. Stained glass artists also create Tiffany-style lamps, which are always increasing in popularity and value. Other stained glass items that an artist can create are kaleidoscopes, clocks, lamp bases and holiday ornaments.

Making stained glass involves cutting pieces of glass and then fitting and soldering the glass into metal frames. Artists usually work from pattern designs when creating projects. Stained glass work takes patience, skill and creativity, which is why there are so few of these artists. Stained glass artists are able to get good money for their beautiful, handcrafted works. Most stained glass artists work in studios or in their home workshops.

Related careers—The etching process leaves a permanent, frosty pattern on glass. Glass etching can be incorporated into stained glass projects or done entirely on its own on items such as mirrors and glassware. Glass can be etched quickly using an etching solution with stencils.

Training

To become a stained glass artist you must get some training to learn the special techniques involved with the craft. In the beginning, it may be difficult to make a good living with stained glass, but after learning how to create breathtaking works, the artist will find him- or herself overloaded with work. There are training programs available for beginners through some community colleges. Most artists start out as apprentices under an established artist, until they learn the trade. There are pattern books available through stained glass suppliers, and kits for beginners.

For more information contact

Franklin Art Glass
222 East Sycamore Street
Columbus, OH 43206
1-800-848-7683
Stained glass supplies and books

Warner Crivellaro Stained Glass
1855 Weaversville Road
Allentown, PA 18103
1-800-523-4242
Stained glass starter kits, supplies, lamp bases and books

Rockler Woodworking
4365 Willow Drive
Medina, MN 55340-9701
1-800-279-4441
Mail order woodworking and etching supplies, ask for catalog

Recommended Reading
    Stained Glass Craft Made Simple, James McDonell, Dover
Publications, 1985

Suncatchers Stained Glass Patternbook, Connie Eaton, Dover Publications, 1987

Traditional Glassworking Techniques, Paul Hasluck, Dover Publications, 1988

• TAXIDERMIST •

Career Description
A taxidermist is a professional who prepares and preserves the skins of animals and artistically stuffs and mounts them in lifelike form. Taxidermists know how to fit skins around forms, mount projects and preserve skins and furs.

Career Opportunities
Most taxidermists operate their own shops and do freelance work for clients who want to preserve animals.

Museums—Many museums hire taxidermists to preserve unusual and rare species of animals. Some museums keep preserved endangered species, while others preserve unusual animals like Trigger, Roy Roger's famous horse, and "Moo Moo," a two-headed cow from the 1930s.

Hunters—Hunters who want to preserve their game are among the taxidermist's main clientele.

Tanning—Taxidermists are often hired to tan hides. Tanning is a process by which animal skins are cleaned and processed into leather.

Other crafts—Taxidermists can make many other crafts, such as bearskin rugs, antler chandeliers and other projects that are big sellers in specialty shops. One taxidermist created the "Jackalope," which was a mounted rabbit head with antelope antlers and a small plaque that told the "history" of the created species. He sold hundreds of "Jackalopes" to tourists in one season.

Training

There is no license required to become a taxidermist, although new taxidermists must learn proper preservation techniques. There are courses, books and videos available to learn the art of taxidermy.

For more information contact

The Northwestern School of Taxidermy
J.W. Elwood Supply Company, Inc.
P.O. Box 3507
Omaha, NE 68103-3507
(402) 342-2362
Correspondence courses in taxidermy, career information and supplies

Van Dyke's Supply
P.O. Box 278
Woonsocket, SD 57385-0278
(605) 796-4425
Taxidermy supplies, kits, instructional books and videos

· TAX PREPARER ·

Career Description

A tax preparer is a professional who prepares income tax statements for individuals and businesses. Tax preparers help clients fill out forms, organize their receipts, claim dependents and other exemptions and total up deductions. Taxes can now be filed electronically and tax preparers can get "rapid refunds" for their clients.

Career Opportunities

There are many opportunities for trained tax preparers. With the constantly changing tax laws and confusing forms to fill out, trained tax preparers can save their clients time, money and frustration. Everyone who works, owns a business or makes income must file tax returns.

Most tax preparers operate their own businesses, but a few work for tax preparation companies. The tax preparer's busy season is from January to April 15 every year, when everyone is scrambling to get a return completed.

Tax preparers get a lot of repeat business from their satisfied clients who return year after year, often referring their friends as well. This is a great business to operate from your home office.

Training

To become a tax preparer you must know how to file tax returns and be familiar with the tax laws. You can take a course at a community college to learn this career or you may complete a correspondence program. There is no licensing or registration required to become a tax preparer *except* in the state of California. If you are a California resident, you must be at least eighteen years old and have completed a tax preparing program approved by the administrator of the California Tax Preparer Program before you are eligible to take a registration test.

Recommended Reading

Barron's Dictionary of Tax Terms, Barron Publishing, 1994

· TRADE SHOW COORDINATOR ·

Career Description

Trade shows are large conventions, public and private, where many companies display their products and/or services at booths to generate more business. A trade show coordinator is a person hired by a business to coordinate, design and handle all of the logistics of appearing at a trade show.

Career Opportunities

There are many types of trade shows that different types of businesses attend, such as computer shows, home improvement shows, gift shows, book shows, job fairs, state and county fairs and special industry trade shows.

Each company that participates in a trade show rents a space and sets up a display to attract people to look at the company's services or products.

Many companies hire freelance trade show coordinators in order to get a professional booth. Coordinators may handle booth design, signs, promotional material, product displays, demonstrations and games and contests, and may even work at the booth for the duration of the trade show. Coordinators help their clients choose a display within the client's budget.

Training

There is no training or licensing required to become a trade show coordinator. The best way to learn the business is to visit booths at trade shows and gather information from companies and representatives. Find out how long it takes them to set up, where they had their booth backdrop and signs made, and so on. Send out mailings to local businesses advertising that you will design and set up their booth for them.

Recommended Reading

How to Be a Weekend Entrepreneur, Making Money at Craft Fairs, Trade Shows & Swap Meets, Susan Ratliff, Marketing Methods Press, 1991

· USED CAR INSPECTOR ·

Career Description

A used car inspector is a person who checks out used vehicles for people before they buy.

Career Opportunities

Often, when buying a used car, people take the car to their mechanic first to have it checked out. Many used cars are sold by private parties in "as is" condition, with no guarantees or warranties. A used car inspector takes the place of the mechanic and travels to his or her clients. An inspector helps clients make good decisions and avoid buying mistakes. A good inspector can also help clients negotiate the price by pointing out problems.

Used car inspection is a very new career that can be started on a part-time basis. A good place to advertise this service is in the used car section of newspapers. Most people will call on Saturdays and Sundays, as these are the most popular days for car buying. Inspectors never guarantee the vehicle they are inspecting; clients pay them only for their honest opinion and advice.

Private parties—Used car inspectors most often work for individuals who want to make sure that the used car they are considering buying is not a lemon. They call the inspector, who comes down to the place the car is and gives an overall inspection of the vehicle and consults the client on whether or not it is a good deal.

Businesses—Small businesses in particular use inspectors when buying used vehicles, such as vans and trucks, for their business. One business hired a used car inspector to locate four used vans for purchase. The inspector called private party ads in the paper and visited vehicle auctions and found four good used vans for the business within two weeks.

Training

There is no license required to become a used car inspector. Used car inspectors must know about cars in order to give their clients sound advice. A background as a mechanic is helpful, but not necessary. New inspectors who don't know much about cars should take classes offered at community colleges in auto repair and maintenance or work in a repair shop as an apprentice.

Recommended Reading

All About Your Car, David Kline and Jamie Robertson, Dimi Press, 1996

Chilton's Auto Repair Manual, Chilton—Annual publication about auto repair

Kelley Blue Book Price Manual—Kelley Blue Book—Bi-monthly publication of new and used car wholesale and retail prices

· VENDING MACHINE REPAIRER ·

Career Description

A vending machine repairer maintains, installs and repairs coin-operated vending machines and games.

The first vending machines were patented in 1886 and dispensed items such as postcards and gum. Throughout the years vending machines have improved in design, and began gaining popularity in the 1950s. Today, vending machines can be found in every city in stores, Laundromats, restaurants, airports, hospitals, arcades—almost everywhere you find people. Vending machines offer drinks, snacks, detergent, change, stamps, toys, sandwiches and many other items. Vending machines do break down and need expert repair people to service and maintain them. This business is rapidly expanding and will continue to do so in the coming years.

Career Opportunities

Most vending machine technicians work freelance and establish their own service routes with owners of machines. Some technicians work as employees for vending machine repair companies. You may also buy and service your own machines to make extra profit.

Training

There is no licensing required to become a vending machine technician. There are courses you can take to learn the trade, or you can apprentice with an established repair person.

For more information contact

National Automatic Merchandising Association (NAMA)
20 North Wacker Drive
Chicago, IL 60606
(312) 346-0370
Information about careers repairing vending machines

Recommended Reading

Automatic Merchandiser, 1233 Janesville Avenue, Ft. Atkinson, WI 53538, 1-800-547-7377—Trade magazine for the vending machine industry

Vending Times, 1375 Broadway, 6th Floor, New York, NY 10018, (212) 302-4700—Monthly magazine for the vending machine industry

· WARDROBE CONSULTANT ·

Career Description
A wardrobe consultant is a person who helps others decide what clothing is best suited for them. Consultants help their clients determine what colors and styles look best.

Career Opportunities
Consultants help their clients organize their closets and get rid of outdated clothing. They also may accompany clients when shopping for a new wardrobe. Good wardrobe consultants can determine what articles of clothing their clients need to buy and where to shop for them. Consultants also help their clients put outfits together and teach them how to accessorize their clothing with shoes, scarves, jewelry, handbags, belts and hats.

The clientele of wardrobe consultants are usually affluent women and men who want to look their best and be fashionably dressed. Another group who hire consultants is celebrities and corporate executives who are trying to promote a particular image or who just don't have the time to hassle with their clothing.

One consultant offers her clients an initial wardrobe makeover and then makes visits once or twice a year to help her clients update their clothing.

Training
There is no training required to become a wardrobe consultant. There are many books available on fashion and colors. A wardrobe consultant can keep up with current fashions by reading fashion magazines and attending fashion shows.

Recommended Reading

The Language of Color, Dorthee L. Mella, Warner Books, 1988

Style, Elsa Klensch, Berkley Publishing, 1995

· WILL WRITER ·

Career Description

A will writer is a person who writes the legal documents that disseminate the property of clients after death.

Career Opportunities

Most people don't like to think about writing a will, but failure to do so can mean losing control of where and to whom property and assets are distributed.

Will writers help their clients draft the will document, which can be a confusing task for the average person. Will writers are familiar with estate laws in their states and know how to correctly draft wills.

Wills should contain the name of the person the will is for and instructions for paying debts, appointing heirs, trustees and guardians; distribution of property and money and funeral arrangements. Everything that the client wishes to be included in the will must be in writing.

Once the will is drafted, most states require that three witnesses (usually nonbeneficiaries) sign each page of the will. These witnesses may be called upon later in probate court to testify to the validity of the will. Only one copy of the will should exist, and it should be kept in a safe place until after death. No changes can be made to the will. If a client wishes changes, a new will must be written and the old document destroyed.

Training

There is no license required to write wills. Will writers should know the laws in their state pertaining to wills and estates. There are many books and computer software programs available to learn about drafting wills.

Recommended Reading

The E-Z Legal Guide: Last Will & Testament, The E-Z Legal Guide: Living Trust, The E-Z Legal Guide: Living Will, E-Z Legal Forms, Inc., 1995

The Jacoby & Meyers Guide to Wills and Estates, Gail J. Koff, Henry Holt and Company, Inc., 1991

The Quick and Legal Will Book, Dennis Clifford, Nolo Press, 1995

· WINDOW DRESSER ·

Career Description

A window dresser is a person hired by retail shops and businesses to create and set up merchandise displays in their windows. Many shops, particularly large department stores, frequently hire freelance window dressers to design effective displays that attract attention and customers to their stores. Window dressers are very creative and keep portfolios of their work.

Career Opportunities

Large department stores hire window dressers to create window displays in their front windows and to do display work inside the store. Dressers choose backgrounds, furniture, mannequins, clothing, accessories and merchandise, and arrange it in a way that creates an attractive scene or display.

Many smaller retail shops, such as toy stores, hardware stores, clothing stores and furniture stores, hire window dressers to create attractive displays and generate more business. A shop owner may want to capture a particular theme with the display or may leave all the decisions entirely up to the dresser.

Window painting is a related profession that tends to be a seasonal business, especially around the winter holiday season. Painters use water-based paint to paint holiday greetings, pictures and scenes on clients' windows. Nearly every type of business may have their windows painted, from department stores to gas stations. The busy season starts in mid-November.

Training

There is no training necessary to become a window dresser. Window dressers have to be creative. A good way to start is to look at shop windows in your area and contact local business owners. Fashion and home decorating magazines will give the new window dresser lots of ideas. To build a professional portfolio of photos, offer your first few clients discounted fees for dressing their windows.

· WOODWORKER ·

Career Description

A woodworker is a person who handcrafts projects from wood

Career Opportunities

There are many projects that can be crafted from wood. I will cover a few of the best-selling possibilities in this section.

Humidors—Humidors are special containers that keep the right amount of moisture inside for storing cigars. These containers or boxes are made of wood and lined with velvet. Humidity gauges are installed to give proper humidity readings. These boxes can be crafted from wood, usually cedar, and sold for several hundred dollars each depending upon beauty and craftsmanship.

Kaleidoscopes—Kaleidoscopes are wooden devices, usually tubes, that have mirrors and bits of colored glass and plastic inside, an eyepiece at one end and a translucent surface at the other. When one looks through the hole and turns the device, colorful, changing patterns are formed. Decorative and treasured kaleidoscopes can be made from special kits and sold for $100 and up.

Music boxes and jewelry boxes—Beautiful music and jewelry boxes can be made from wood. Music-playing devices can be bought to play certain songs and installed in the box. These decorative boxes are lined with velvet and may have inlaid glass or mirror tops.

Steamer trunks—Old fashioned wooden trunks can be crafted from wood using an antique pattern. These trunks are beautiful as well as practical and can be used to store blankets, books and memorabilia, and for traveling. Steamer trunks have brass or nickel fittings and can be made out of many types of wood. A professionally crafted trunk can sell for several hundred dollars.

Coffee mills—Old-fashioned coffee mills and grinders are wooden boxes with a coffee grinding device on top. Coffee beans are placed in the cast-iron grinder and the ground coffee removed through a small drawer in the box. These highly decorative and useful mills are always popular items.

Carousel Animal Carving—Carousel animals are carved from high-quality basswood and painted in great detail, before being mounted on brass poles and sold, mainly to amusement parks and collectors. There are only a handful of artists in the world practicing this nearly lost art. The price of carousel animals depends upon the skill of the artist and the aesthetics of the piece. They can sell for $1,000 on up to $12,000.

Other projects—Some of the other projects that can be crafted from wood include walking canes, fountain pens, candle holders, furniture, children's toys, mirrors and picture frames.

Training

Woodworkers must know how to use saws, lathes, sanders, levels, drills, clamps and other woodworking tools. You can take woodworking classes, which are available through some community colleges and vocational schools, or you can read books and watch videos on the subject. Other woodworkers learn their trades by apprenticing for established craftsmen.

For more information contact

The School of Carousel Horse Carving
2122 West Midwood
Anaheim, CA 92804
(714) 635-0917
Classes and personal instruction taught by master carver W. P. Wilcox. Call for class schedules and seminar dates.

Van Dyke's Restoration
P.O. Box 278
Woonsocket, SD 57385
1-800-843-3320
Woodworking supplies, books and videos, request catalog

The Woodworkers' Store
4365 Willow Drive
Medina, MN 55340-9701
1-800-279-4441
Mail-order woodworking supplies, humidor kits, kaleidoscope kits, jewelry and music box kits, coffee mill kits, furniture plans, toy plans and etching supplies, ask for catalog

Recommended Reading

American Woodworker Woodworking Techniques, Rodale Press, 1988

The Art and Craft of Carving Wood, Antony Denning, Running Press, 1994—A helpful resource for carvers

The Complete Guide to Professional Woodworking, Ben Calhoun, Prentice-Hall, 1989

The Kaleidoscope Book, Sterling Publishing Company, 1995

Reader's Digest Book of Skills and Tools, Reader's Digest Books, 1993

Woodworking Techniques: Tips and Projects from a Master Craftsman, William B. Bigelow, Tab Books, 1989

· WORD PROCESSOR ·

Career Description

A word processor is a person who prepares documents or does data entry on a computer. This career is a good part-time venture that can be operated from home.

Career Opportunities

These days, many companies hire outside secretarial help to cut down on overhead expenses. Some of the assignments a word processor might take on are résumés, brochures, novels, scripts and data entry.

A good example of an assignment is a small service company who had been in business over fifteen years. They wanted to transfer all of their customers' names from paper receipts onto their new computer system, but didn't have the time or manpower to do it themselves. They hired a freelance word processor to input all of the data. The assignment was completed in three weeks.

Training

There is no training required to enter this field, but a word processor must know how to type and must own a computer. Most word processors are able to type forty-five to seventy words per minute. Typing and computer classes are offered at community colleges, and there are many books available about starting a word processing service.

Recommended Reading

How to Set Up and Run a Typing Service, Donna Clark Goodrich, John Wiley & Sons, 1983

How to Start a Word Processing Business at Home, John J. Branson III, Spectrum Books, 1985

Word Processing Profits at Home, Peggy Glenn, Aames-Allen Publishing, 1989

THREE
Organization

If you choose to become a freelance professional, you will need to be able to manage yourself, your time and your actions. A freelance career is much like owning your own business. You have to work hard to succeed and get it off the ground.

Organization is an important factor for freelance professionals. Time, money and records must be kept in an orderly manner. Here are a few tips to help you stay on top of things.

MANAGING YOUR TIME

When you're working at home or for yourself, it can be tempting to do other things besides work, such as housework, talking to friends, watching a little TV or taking a two-hour lunch. After all, there is no boss or manager hanging over your shoulder, watching your every move.

As a freelance professional, you should be able to work the hours you want, but make sure that you actually balance out the work and play hours in your life. Working for yourself requires self-discipline. Poor time management is the major downfall of freelancers. You can beat the odds by setting up a working schedule and sticking to it. Decide what hours you will work and adhere to your own schedule. You may want to work from noon to 8 P.M., or you may want to break up your schedule into odd hours, from 9 to noon and then 6 to midnight. Do whatever works for you, but remember that a scheduled, orderly environment is a sane environment.

Keep daily to do lists. At the end of *every day*, take ten minutes to write down tasks that need to be accomplished tomorrow. By listing tomorrow's activities on paper, you are actually freeing up your mind and attention and will find it easier to unwind. Write down everything from your grocery shopping to your big meeting with a new client. Once you've listed everything that needs to be accomplished, prioritize the items on your list using 1's, 2's and 3's. 1's are written next to those tasks that are the most important and absolutely must be done, 2's are written next to those tasks that need to be done but are not as important as the 1's, and 3's are written next to the minor tasks that can be done as you find time during the day.

MANAGING YOUR MONEY

Good record-keeping skills are an essential part of running a successful freelance business. Besides being necessary for your taxes, financial records are vital so that you, the owner, can maintain statistics and always know where you stand financially. Always keep your financial records updated. Never allow yourself to get behind.

CHECK REGISTERS

You will have to set up a checking account for your business. Some freelancers make the mistake of using their personal checking accounts for business purposes, which can project a cloudy picture. Set up a separate checking account for your business *only* and *never* mix your business and personal expenses. Keep your business check register updated at all times. When you set up your business bank account, order a checkbook that has a receipt log. Every time you write a check, record who the check was made out to, for what, the date, the check number and your remaining balance. Don't forget to record bank charges and withdrawls. If you do this, you will always know how much money is available. Failure to do this will result in chaos.

RECEIPTS

Always keep receipts for all of your business expenses and file them every week. Business expenses are generally considered money that you've spent in order to keep your business going. Examples of such expenses are vehicle expenses, equipment, supplies, travel and anything else that is a legitimate cost incurred by your business. Make up a ledger or sheet that lists what each receipt was for, the date and the amount, and file it with your receipts every week. This will help you keep track of your spending, and your files will be organized when tax time comes around.

If you have to travel with your new career, take along a file and keep all of your receipts in this file. Keep your business expense receipts, such as gas, lodging and food, and sort them out when you get back to your office.

SALES TRANSACTIONS AND RECEIPTS

Whenever you accept money from clients, you are required to give them a receipt. Get some three-part carbon forms made up with your name printed at the top, or use ready-made three-part forms and a rubber stamp. Give the customer the top copy as a receipt and keep the other two for your records. One of your copies should be filed with your weekly receipts, along with a sheet of that week's total income. The other copy should be filed alphabetically in your customer records.

BILLS

At the beginning of every month or week, whichever you prefer, make a sheet that lists every bill that you owe. List who you owe, the amount, what it's for and on what date it is due. Keep the list in a file with your actual bills. Cross off each item as you pay each bill and file your bills at the end of each month.

ACCOUNTS RECEIVABLE

Many freelance professionals grant their clients credit and send out bills for work that has been completed. It is important to keep on top of this to ensure that you are paid. Keep a ledger or a list of all clients who owe you money, when the money is due, how much is due and what service was provided. As your customers pay you, note this in your ledger or cross them off the list, and make a note in their file that the job was paid for. These records can be kept on paper or on computer. Choose the method that you feel most comfortable with.

PROFESSIONAL HELP

In the beginning, you should not need a professional bookkeeper to handle your books. Do as much of your basic bookkeeping as possible yourself. You should be responsible for keeping your daily financial logs in order. This will save you money while you're getting your business off the ground.

The one exception to this is if your business grows beyond what you can handle your first year. At that point, you can reevaluate the situation to determine what you need.

At tax time, you may require outside help from a bookkeeper. Many freelancers have their taxes prepared by a professional each year.

MANAGING YOUR RECORDS

Besides your financial records, you'll need to keep a few other records to keep your business organized and to chart your expansion and growth.

FILES

Keeping organized files will help you run your business smoothly. Investing in a filing cabinet in the beginning is always a good idea. Keep your company records, such as your business license, bank account information, permits and advertising artwork, filed alphabetically. You may need to obtain these files on a moment's notice and will want to have them easily accesible.

CUSTOMER FILES

Keep customer files. Each customer should have his or her own file organized in alphabetical order. All work orders, sales receipts and other information about each client should be found within the file. It is sometimes handy to have the customer's name, address and phone number written on the file for quick reference.

Your customer files should not be neglected. They will serve as a valuable tool for future mailing lists and repeat business.

CHARTING YOUR GROWTH

One of the best ways to have a clear picture of your business at all times is to keep charted records.

At the end of every week, total up all of the income generated that week by your business and mark it above the date on a piece of graph paper. This is your gross income. Take that same weekly figure and deduct all overhead expenses and material and mark the difference on that same piece of graph paper. This is your net profit. You can chart about two months of these statictics on one piece of graph paper and always have a clear picture of your business activity.

You might also want to chart weekly statistics such as number of new clients, number of jobs done or number of advertising pieces delivered to help you see how you're progressing. Your statistics should mirror how your business is doing, and you should always work toward increasing the numbers for positive indicators.

Graphs can also be kept on computer. There are computer programs available that will automatically chart your statistics for you when you input your weekly totals, using a simple chart system like this to detect increases or decreases in stats.

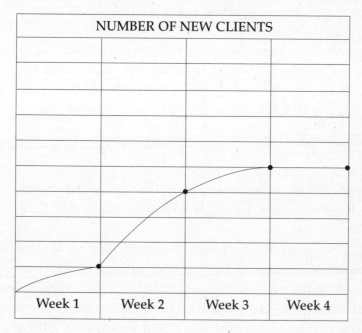

FOUR
Selling Your Products, Your Services and Yourself

No matter what you do in life, you'll have to do some selling to get by. Remember when you wanted to borrow your parent's car as a teenager? This was quite a sales pitch. You had to get your parent to believe that you were capable of driving, you had to negotiate by agreeing to come home by ten and you had to promise to drive safely. Finally, after much persuasion, Dad handed you the keys. No matter who you are or what you do, selling is a part of life. If you're going to be working as a freelance professional, you'll need to polish up on your sales skills. After all, you'll be selling your image, services and products.

I have learned a lot about sales over the years, having started and operated many businesses. I want to share some invaluable selling technology that I've found. In the following section you will learn the selling secrets of Harry Frisch, award-winning salesman. Read the data and apply it in sales and in life.

"Selling" is defined as the art of persuading another to firmly commit to acquiring an item, service or idea. The art and technique of "sales" are the same as those of "persuasion." So even if you have no desire to become an actual salesperson yourself, you will, by learning the theory and application of the art of persuasion, become empowered to improve your life in any and all sectors in which you wish to increase your influence.

Selling is made up of a specific set of skills which nearly anyone can learn to apply effectively. The sales process has five steps, which are in a particular sequence. By creatively applying this sequence of steps, you will instantly improve your ability to make the sale.

Salespeople are not "born that way," but rather become that way by developing their basic skills through study and application. The process of a sale is made up of a specific set of skills and procedures that can be identified, learned, practiced and perfected.

As in any profession, the more aptitude one has for the required skills, the less difficulty one is apt to experience in mastering that field. But my experience has shown me that nearly anyone with enough drive and perseverance can learn and perfect the skills and learn and adopt the winning attitudes it takes to be a professional salesperson.

Some salespeople may have had a better start than others, but . . . great salespeople were not born that way. They got there the old-fashioned way: they worked at it. So can you.

WHAT IS A SALE?

A sale is as a five-step process beginning with finding someone to sell something to and concluding with a firm commitment from that person to acquire that which is being sold.

The sequence of the sales process is

1. *Prospecting*—locating a prospective buyer
2. *Opening*—getting the prospect into communication
3. *Qualifying*—discovering certain relevant data about the prospect
4. *Presenting*—enlightening the prospect about the product or service
5. *Closing*—getting the prospect's firm commitment to acquire the product or service

Why are these five steps *the* five steps and why in *this* particular sequence? The workable structure of a sale is not what it is because I say it is, or for any other such arbitrary reason. The second step of the sequence of a sale has to have the first step in place in order for the second step to be properly and stably erected. The third step needs the second step in place for that third step to take place properly. And so on, all the way up to the fifth and final step, which needs the fourth step in place to stably support it.

So this sequence a sale follows is the sequence it would logically need to follow in order to do what it is supposed to do—to result in a sale!

It is sometimes easier to grasp the logic of this sequence by viewing it backwards. Let's take a look at the sale starting with where it ends (with a successfully completed sale) and work our way back to the beginning (finding someone to sell something to). The Sales Process in reverse:

5. CLOSING

What you are ultimately striving for in the sales process is to make the sale, to *close* it, to get a firm commitment from the prospect. This is a solid agreement that the prospect will acquire from you whatever product or service you have been offering him or her.

4. PRESENTING

Before a prospect can be expected to firmly commit to acquiring your product, service or idea, he or she would first need to somehow be introduced to it, to learn about it, experience it, be told about it, be shown it, be *presented* it. The prospect would need to be presented it in such a way that he or she sees the value and benefit of it *to the prospect*, a value and benefit *at least equal* to the price he or she is agreeing to exchange for it.

3. QUALIFYING

Before you can effectively and credibly present to the prospect how the features of this product of yours will be of proper benefit and value to him or her, you must first learn from the prospect what it is about the prospect and his or her needs and wants that this product might satisfy. Similarly, before you can effectively strategize your campaign of exactly what, when and how you are going to present your wares to this particular prospect, you will need to learn what his or her readiness and ability are to experience and acquire whatever it is that you are selling. This discovering of relevant needs, wants, readiness and ability is called *qualifying*.

2. OPENING

Now, before you can get the prospect to tell you anything about anything, you've got to get him or her willing to communicate with you. Before you can get the prospect to truthfully tell you about him- or herself and about the needs, wants and limitations of the prospect's life, you've got to get the prospect to at least have some basic trust in you. Establishing this communication with basic trust is called *opening*.

1. PROSPECTING

Before you can begin to get the prospect into any kind of communication with you at all, you first have to locate him or her. Locating the prospect is called *prospecting*.

There are a few key points to selling that I would like to note here.

THE 101 BEST FREELANCE CAREERS

1. Selling is made up of a specific set of skills, which nearly anyone can learn to apply effectively.

2. The ability to smoothly lead your prospects through the process of a sale is developed through good training and practice.

3. *Qualifying* is the process of discovering your prospect's needs and wants as well as the process of discovering your prospect's readiness and ability to acquire your product or services.

4. The earlier steps, which lead to the close, are the very foundation upon which the close is based. The more thoroughly you understand and handle these earlier steps, the less effort you will need to devote to the close and the more overall control you'll be able to maintain over your sales.

5. It is far more effective for your prospect to see for him- or herself how a product will satisfy the prospect's needs than for you to just tell the prospect about it.

6. How attentively you are able to listen is as important if not more important than how effectively you are able to speak.

7. It is a winning practice to allow your prospect to control the forward motion of the sale whenever he or she is moving it in the right direction at optimum speed.

8. While some salespeople are quite unethical (as are a minority in any profession), most are service-oriented people of goodwill, striving to do the right thing.

WHAT SHOULD I CHARGE FOR MY SERVICES?

If you're going to be working as a freelance professional, you'll have to determine what to charge for your services before you can begin to sell. You'll want to charge fair fees that will encourage clients to use you and/or your services. Your fees must also allow you to turn a profit that you're satisfied with. Take a look at the categories below.

SELLING YOUR PRODUCTS, YOUR SERVICES AND YOURSELF

TIME AND EXPERTISE

What do you consider your time to be worth an hour, a day, a week, a month or on this project or assignment? Will your client be saving money by using you? If yes, how much?

WHAT ARE YOUR OVERHEAD COSTS?

Take a look at how much it costs you to operate your business. Include your rent, electricity, phone bills, travel expenses (gas, vehicle wear and tear, car payments and insurance), advertising costs and anything else that applies. Add this up monthly, then break it down weekly, daily and hourly.

WHAT WILL YOUR MATERIALS COST?

If this is applicable, figure out how much money you'll have to spend to get the job done right and be sure to budget it into your fee.

WHAT DOES THE COMPETITION CHARGE?

One of the best ways to get a feel for the "going rates" is to make a few phone calls to your competition. What are the lows and the highs? Find out what similar professionals are charging for their services.

HOW SHOULD I CHARGE?

Many freelance professionals pose this question in the beginning. The answer varies with each profession, project and assignment. We'll cover the different types of billing here:

Hourly—Your client pays you on an hourly basis for your services.
Daily—Your client pays you for a day's work.

Weekly—Your client pays you once a week for your services.
Per assignment—Your client pays you to complete an assignment or service.

You may arrange for partial payment at the start of the job and the remainder when the job is complete. Be careful to do a correct time estimate if you're being paid this way. Ask yourself how many hours or days it will take to complete the job, figure out the lump sum based on your hourly or daily fees.

FIVE

How to Advertise

Advertising simply means making your products and services known to the public. You may have the best product or service in the world, but if people don't know about it, you'll soon find yourself out of business.

The biggest mistake that freelance professionals and business owners make is failure to advertise. The failure to advertise and make themselves known is the direct cause of the complete failure of many businesses and careers. Other causes are poor service, unethical business practices and bad products.

Many new business owners and freelancers don't understand the importance of advertising until it is too late.

A perfect example of this phenomenon is a man who opens up a retail clothing store and puts most of his money into his inventory, figuring that the customers will just find him—after all, he is selling the best clothing in town! "Who has money to advertise!" he tells himself. So he sits in his shop and twiddles his thumbs, waiting for customers to come in. Sure, a few come in here and there, but he isn't getting enough business to pay the bills. He begins to blame his failure on the "neighborhood" or "the clothing store down the street" and becomes bitter and angry. By the next month, the landlord is knocking on his door, demanding the overdue rent. The store owner can't pay his bills and is about to go out of business. He panics! So he scrapes up his last few dollars and gets a few giant neon orange banners printed saying, "Going Out of Business Sale! 50% Off Entire Inventory!" Suddenly the customers begin pouring into the store! If he's smart, he'll recognize the importance of advertising and be able to keep his shop open. Had he hung neon banners in the first place, he would have saved himself a lot of headaches and possibly his business. This is just one example of failure to advertise. Never underestimate the power of making yourself and your products known.

Advertising applies to all freelance professionals and businesses, no matter what kind of services they provide or what kind of products they sell. The public must be made aware of what you've got to offer.

Think of advertising as a vehicle that will take your career or business down the road to success.

Advertising is communication. You must communicate about your products and services to your potential clients. Of course, you may be rejected, but that's all part of the freelance game.

WAYS TO ADVERTISE

There are many ways to get the word out about your services and products. I will list a few here.

YELLOW PAGES

Your local Yellow Pages can bring you a gold mine of business. When you set up your business phone lines with the phone company, ask them about advertising rates in the phone book. You may want to start out with a one-line ad under the correct heading, or you may want to invest in a display ad. A representative from the yellow pages will help you design and create an effective ad. Remember that most people look in the phone book when they need a service or product.

DIRECT MAIL

Direct mailings can bring you lots of business. In order to put together an effective mailing, figure out who your potential clients are. You can buy specific lists of certain types of people from mailing list companies. These companies have lists compiled and categorized by demographics such as income level, or sorted into groups such as home owners, doctors, pet owners, pool owners, computer owners and hundreds of others. Mailing list companies can be found in your yellow pages under "Mailing Lists."

REFERRALS AND NETWORKING

The best way to get business is by word-of mouth. A customer who has found you through the recommendation of another is more likely to use your service or product, because they have already heard good things about you. You can get referrals from previous customers by asking them if they know of anyone who might also need your services. You can also get referrals from other professionals and businesses who know you and will recommend your services to their customers. Good ways to meet other professionals who will recommend you is to attend business mixers, visit businesses and join networking clubs. Always have a stack of your business cards with you to give away.

SIGNS

If you have an office in a business district, get an attractive sign made up so that people can find you. You'll be surprised by the foot traffic that a sign will attract. You can also get your name, logo and phone number painted on your work vehicle or have a magnetic sign made, which is a temporary sign that will stick to a vehicle. This will instantly turn your car or van into a rolling advertisement for you. You can also have personalized bumper stickers and license plate frames made up to put on your vehicle.

FLYERS

A flyer is an advertisement or brochure that can be distributed to potential customers, stating your name and phone number and briefly telling about your products or services. Flyers are generally effective and can be passed out door-to-door to homes or businesses in the neighborhoods in which you wish to work. Flyers can also be posted on notice boards.

BUSINESS CARDS AND PROMOTIONAL ITEMS

Business cards are one of the most effective ways to get clients. Be sure to get your business cards printed right away when you start a new career or business. Cards can be handed out to potential clients or left with people who will refer you. Besides helping generate business, business cards will make you look professional and established. You may also have novelty promotional items made up to advertise your services and products, such as pens, notepads, magnets, key chains, bumper stickers, T-shirts and tote bags. Look in the Yellow Pages under "Promotional Items" or "Advertising" to find companies that will print your name and phone number on such items.

If you're selling a product, make sure that your name and number is attached to the product with a label or tag so that customers know how to reach you for reorders. A good example of this type of advertising is a computer consultant in Los Angeles who gives each of his clients a mouse pad with his name and number printed on it.

KEEPING IN TOUCH

In today's competitive world, a little extra effort will get you loyal customers and more repeat business. Customers appreciate a little recognition and personal attention. Sending thank-you cards to your clients is a great way to let them know that they're appreciated. Take the time to say thanks and to sign your name. This action will build you a loyal base of repeat customers and will make them more likely to refer their friends and family to you. Write letters to your customer base every year to let them know that you remember them and to fill them in on what you're doing.

HOW TO CREATE AN EFFECTIVE ADVERTISEMENT

Now that you have seen a few ways to advertise, let's take a look at how you can create an effective ad that will generate business. We'll be looking at a few very important aspects of creating the ideal ad, and I'll show you how to set up a knock-'em-dead marketing piece. This section focuses on you and your new career and will answer some important questions about how to effectively communicate who you are and what services you provide. Learn how to develop advertising buttons and slogans that customers will respond to. Read and fill in the blanks in the following section.

1. **Who** am I?
Figure out who you are. What is your name? What is your profession?

Your name   **Your professional title**

_____   _____

Example—John Smith, Computer Tutor, or Joan Blackwell, Facialist

1A. **Who** will use my services or products?

Figure out who specifically will use your products and services.

The people that will need my services or products are

_____

_____

_____

Example—Bill's Pool Cleaning would answer "People with pools, community centers, hotels and motels." Nancy's Word Processing Service would answer "People in Southern California without computers, and businesses who need someone to make up brochures."

2. **What** will be needed from me by my clients?

Figure out exactly what your clients will need and want from you, your services or your products. These may be things like fast service, reliability, good products, knowledge, experience or great prices.

What is needed?

_____

_____

_____

Example—Smith's Acupressure would answer "Good service, knowledge, professional attitude and relief from pain." Don's Fishing Tackle would answer "Handcrafted fishing tackle, good prices and mail order."

3. **When** or in what situation will my customers need me?

Figure out when your services will be needed. If you have a résumé service, you will be needed when people need to find work, or if you're a computer tutor, they'll need you when they have questions about computers.

When or in what situation will I be needed?

_____

_____

_____

Example—Mark's Organization Service would answer "When people need to get organized." Jimmy's Chimney Inspection Service would answer "When people want to know if their chimneys are safe."

4. **Where** will I be needed?
Figure out at what locations and areas you and your products or services will be needed. You may be needed at schools, at businesses, at your home, in your city, state, town or nationwide.

Where will I be needed?

_____

_____

_____

Example—Betty's Antique Repairing would answer "In Jackson, Wyoming." Dave's Pilot Service would answer "Wherever clients need me to go."

5. **Why** would my clients call me?
Figure out why your potential clients would use your products or services and list as many reasons as you can.

Why would they call me?

_____

_____

_____

Example—Jim's Floral Design would answer "Because I know how to make beautiful flower arrangements." Jack the Paramedic would answer "Because I am a highly trained professional in my field."

6. How can I be reached?
How can you be reached by potential clients? What is your phone number, fax number, address and hours of business?

How can I be reached?
Name   **Phone number/Fax number**   **Address**
_____   _____   _____

What are my hours of business?

_____

Here are a few examples of how others have used their answers to create advertising buttons and slogans:

  1. **Who**—John Bates, Fishing Tackle Maker
1A. **Who**—Serving all fisherman
  2. **What**—Experienced, custom work done
  3. **When**—When you're ready to catch the "big one"!
  4. **Where**—Serving fishermen nationwide
  5. **Why**—Come to me for the best tackle around!
  6. **How**—Call 1-800-BIG-FISH, 9 A.M. to 9 P.M. every day.

Another Example:

  1. **Who**—Kelly Kane, Clock Repairer
1A. **Who**—Anyone with a broken clock

2. **What**—Expert clock repairs, speedy service and competitive rates
3. **When**—Does your clock needs a tune-up or repair?
4. **Where**—In Washoe County
5. **Why**—I can fix any clock
6. **How**—Call (702) 555-5555 or visit the shop at 1234 Easy Street, Reno, NV 55555.

SIX

The Home Office

Most freelance professionals work out of their home offices and workshops. Many freelance careers require minimal work space and storage. A spare bedroom, garage or section of a living room will usually suffice when you're first starting out, and will keep your overhead costs down.

Make sure that you have adequate storage space available for supplies, records, files, tools and equipment. If your new career requires more work space than you have available, or a professional office environment, you'll need to consider leasing an office.

FURNISHINGS AND SUPPLIES

Whether or not you'll be operating from home, you'll probably need to buy a few office essentials to get started. Buying used office furniture can save you a lot of money, and you can buy your office supplies at warehouse-type stores.

The following checklist was designed to help you take inventory and estimate your start-up costs. You may not need everything on the list and may already have some of the items. Remember to keep receipts for everything you buy for your office.

THE HOME OFFICE

SUPPLIES CHECKLIST

ITEM	DO I HAVE IT?	WILL I NEED IT?	PRICE
desk or worktable			
chairs			
computer/printer			
filing cabinets			
bookshelves			
fax machine/fax paper			
telephone			
copier			
in/out baskets			
lamp			
pens/pencils			
paper			
stapler/staples			
calculator			
paper clips			
scissors			
tape			
glue			
correction fluid			
computer disks			
envelopes			
file folders			
Rolodex			
letterhead			
business cards			

WORKING WITH CHILDREN IN THE HOUSE

Many freelance professionals who have home offices often have another dilemma: children. Children need attention and they need it often. Many professionals have chosen to work at home so they can spend more time with the children. Working in the same house with young children running about can be done and it can be done smoothly.

If you plan to care for children while working, be sure to choose a career that can be started and stopped often (like every fifteen to thirty minutes). I believe that children take priority over work and careers, and I schedule my work around my child. If I can't be available to dedicate enough time and attention, I make other arrangements.

BABIES AND INFANTS

Many new parents have chosen to work at home to be with their babies. Babies are quite easy to take care of while working from a home office, since they tend to sleep more then older children. A playpen or crib can be placed in the office with you or a bouncing seat can be hung from the doorway.

TODDLERS

It can be quite an ordeal to work and care for a curious toddler at the same time. Many freelancer parents set up their work spaces so that the child is in a safe environment. Books, lamps, files and other items of interest to toddlers are placed out of sight and out of reach. Snacks and toys can be kept in the work space to keep little tykes occupied. Take meal breaks with your child and schedule regular naps.

OLDER CHILDREN

Whether your child isn't old enough for school yet or school is out for the summer, working with older children in the house can be done. Older children are able to understand how to be quiet when you're on the phone and what it means when Mommy or Daddy cannot be disturbed.

Children love to imitate. Give your older child his or her own "work space" well stocked with crayons, paper, books, play telephones and anything else that might resemble your work area. This will keep your child busy for short periods of time and teach him or her early on about work ethics. Other children can be kept busy with games, books, puzzles and videos.

Depending upon their age and skill level, some older children will be able to help you with simple tasks such as stuffing envelopes, filing and cleaning.

PHONES

Unfortunately, children playing and screaming in the background on a telephone call is generally considered unprofessional and can be distracting to you. You don't want clients to think that they're paying you to watch your child and give them a half-done job. So, whenever possible, keep the children quiet while you're on the telephone.

OTHER ALTERNATIVES

If you can't, or don't want to, watch your children while you are working, there are other solutions. The first and most obvious is to take them to day care or hire a housekeeper/nanny. This is often the best solution when your career requires you to be out of the home frequently.

If you can't afford child care, you can take turns baby-sitting with other freelancers. This works quite well for some people. Most often, one freelancer will watch another freelancer's child one day and then will have the other freelancer watch his or her child the next, but you can use whatever schedule works for you. Schedule your outside appointments for the days your child will be out of the home and your letter writing and other home work on days when you'll be baby-sitting. You might also consider working with a partner who has children and would be willing to split up the baby-sitting with you.

SEVEN

Freelancer's Legal Guide

In order to become a successful freelance professional you must run your operation like a business. In the eyes of the law and other governing organizations, freelance professionals, independent contractors and the self-employed are viewed as businesses.

Before you start your new career, it is recommended that you contact an attorney to find out what licenses, permits, insurance, laws and tax requirements apply to you and your new venture. Setting up your operation legally will save you hassles and problems down the road.

Below is a list of permits and licenses that you may need to obtain for your new business or career.

TAXES

Freelancers, independent contractors and those who are self-employed must pay their own federal and state income taxes. You must pay quarterly income taxes to the Internal Revenue Service. You must estimate what your income taxes for the year will be and divide that into four payments. Payments are due on April 15, June 15, September 15 and January 15. If you have underpaid over the course of the year, the remainder is due on the following April 15. Call your local IRS office to request your free copy of their self-employed tax guidelines book.

Self-employed people may deduct office rent (or a percentage of your house payment or home rent if you work from your home), utilities, business travel, education, books and other publications related to your business, work clothing, telephone and fax expenses, office supplies, tools and work equipment, computers, postage, advertising expenses, copying expenses, cleaning supplies and most other genuine work-related expenses. Keep receipts and monthly ledgers of your work expenses.

BUSINESS LICENSES AND DBA

Most cities require business and freelancers to have a business license to operate within the district. You will also need to get a "doing business as" or DBA, which is a statement that allows individuals to operate their business under a fictitious name. Create a DBA name that reflects what your business does. You need to have a DBA in order to open a business bank account. The DBA also specifies if the business is a sole proprietorship, partnership or corporation.

SOLE PROPRIETORSHIP

Most freelance professionals choose to be sole proprietors. Being a sole proprietor means that you are the only owner of the business. You are required to pay taxes on profits received from the business. This type of business can be opened in your personal name or under a business name.

PARTNERSHIP

A partnership is chosen if there is more that one owner of the business and the owners are considered equal unless otherwise specified. If you choose to open this type of business, have a written contract drawn up and notarized. Partners are equally responsible for debt incurred by the business.

CORPORATIONS

Corporations are seperate, legal entities. Setting up a corporation involves more paperwork and usually requires outside legal help. The advantage of having a corporation is that the owners or shareholders are not personally liable for company debts, and creditors of the company can't set claims against their personal assets. The disadvantages are that setting up a corporation can be expensive and complex, and running a small business as a corporation does not always guarantee limited liability from debt collectors.

SELLER'S PERMIT

You must obtain a seller's permit if your business sells tangible property that is subject to state sales tax. If you plan to buy supplies, equipment or merchandise at wholesale prices, you must also have a seller's permit. Seller's permits are free and can be obtained through your State Board of Equalization office.

INSURANCE

You may be required by your state to carry insurance policies for vehicles, products, theft, liability and damage. If you hire employees, you are required to carry a worker's compensation insurance policy and you must deduct payroll taxes from their wages. Contact your insurance agent to ensure that you have adequate coverage.

How to Write a Business Plan

Your new career as a freelance professional should be operated and planned out as if it were a business. Starting a new career or business takes planning. The purpose of a business plan is to help you focus in on your new venture and to systematically turn your dreams and hopes into reality. By writing down every step of your plan, you will be able to see exactly what your goals are and how to acheive them. Business plans can also be used to help raise money from investors and bankers. The section below was designed to help you plan your business and your future.

What is your new career or business?

_____

_____

What services or products will you provide?

_____

_____

_____

Will you start full-time or part-time?

_____

Do you need any special training or knowledge to get started?

_____

If yes, how and when will you get this training or knowledge?

_____
_____
_____

Who will you sell you services or products to?

_____
_____
_____

Who is your competition?

_____
_____
_____

Where will you operate your business from?

_____
_____
_____

What are you hours of operation?

_____

How will you advertise?

_____
_____
_____

How much will you charge for your products or services?

_____

_____
_____

What will your overhead costs be?

_____
_____
_____

What will your start-up expenses be?

_____
_____
_____

What permits, licenses, insurance, etc., do you need to obtain for this career?

_____
_____
_____
_____
_____
_____

When will you start you new career or business?

_____

What is your projected income?

_____